Subverting Hatred

The Challenge of Nonviolence in Religious Traditions

Edited by
Daniel L. Smith-Christopher

Boston Research Center for the 21st Century
November 1998

The Boston Research Center for the 21st Century (BRC) is an
international peace institute founded in 1993 by Daisaku Ikeda, a
Buddhist peace activist and president of Soka Gakkai International,
an association of Buddhist organizations in 128 countries. The
BRC brings together scholars and activists in dialogue on common
values across cultures and religions, seeking in this way to support
an evolving global ethic for a peaceful twenty-first century.
Human rights, nonviolence, ecological harmony, and economic
justice are focal points of the Center's work.

Published by
Boston Research Center for the 21st Century
396 Harvard Street
Cambridge, MA 02138-3924

ISBN 1-887917-02-0
Library of Congress catalogue card number: 98-074371

Style editing by Helen Marie Casey
Copyediting by Kali Saposnick
Desktop publishing by Ralph Buglass
Cover design by The McCoy Group

TABLE OF CONTENTS

PREFACE

"Nonviolence is the first article of my faith. It is also the last article of my creed," Mahatma Gandhi declared in 1922, linking a faith tradition and personal behavior.

In the chapters of *Subverting Hatred: The Challenge of Nonviolence in Religious Traditions*, a gathering of notable authors has focused on the questions: What are the teachings about nonviolence in the world's major religious traditions? How have these teachings been exemplified? The readings, which are compelling, have a particular resonance not only for students of religion but also for all of us whose work is the pursuit of peace. As Daisaku Ikeda observed about the twentieth century in his 1998 peace proposal, *Humanity and the New Millennium: From Chaos to Cosmos:* "Perhaps no other century has been witness to such endless tragedy and human folly; the global environment has been grievously damaged, and the gap between rich and poor is greater than ever."

Religion has always been a refuge and a guide, in good times and in bad. Its teachings have shown us the way to live and have strengthened us when chaos or evil have welled up around us. Further, religious foundations have provided the framework for world leaders as they have roused their followers to action. Yet, ironically, as the writers of this text demonstrate, religious exhortations have been used to justify violent actions, including war, as frequently as they have been used to urge the way of peace. It is an appropriate time, then, for an assessment of our religious traditions and spiritual foundations and an appropriate time to ask how these traditions prepare us to move into the next millennium.

In gratitude for their insights, it gives me particular pleasure to thank our content editor, Daniel Smith-Christopher, and our style editor, Helen Marie Casey. I also wish to thank our scholars and to recommend this collection of essays.

—Virginia Straus
Executive Director
Boston Research Center for the 21st Century

FOREWORD

I am deeply appreciative to the Boston Research Center for the 21st Century for its initiative in exploring new visions for a peaceful twenty-first century. I am also grateful to the prominent scholars who share their wisdom in *Subverting Hatred: The Challenge of Nonviolence in Religious Traditions*. In an era when Earth has tottered on the brink of nuclear annihilation and when internal strife has all too often sundered families and communities, the question of how to transform hatred—moving from animosity to compassion, suspicion to trust, division to unity—is of utmost importance.

We must move from a twentieth century filled with war and violence to a twenty-first century of peace and coexistence. True and lasting peace will be realized only by forging bonds of trust at the deepest level between people.

Each of the religious traditions represented in this book has a rich history, sacred texts and rituals, and inspiring lessons and exemplars. It is crucial to reexamine these for the resources they offer to the theory and practice of nonviolence.

Without blurring the very real distinctions between each tradition, I think it is fair to say that all religions have grown from similar human impulses—the desire to understand the place of human beings in the universe, to come to grips with the mysteries of life and death, and the wish to experience sustained meaning and joy in the face of the inevitability of suffering and loss.

Even more pressing, however, is the need to look forward to the concrete actions and the concrete wisdom that each tradition can bring to bear on the problems facing humankind at this critical juncture. If humanity is to have a future, it must be a shared one, a future of interaction and coexistence among the world's peoples, cultures, and religious traditions.

Writing at the start of the twentieth century, Tsunesaburo Makiguchi, the founding president of the Soka Gakkai, predicted that relations between states would eventually enter a stage of what he termed "humanitarian competition"; that is, they would each strive with each other to see which could offer the greatest hope and happiness to humankind, both within and outside their national boundaries.

I believe that this same model of "humanitarian competition" can be applied to religions. The highest value will be created when each tradition exerts its fullest efforts in a "peace race," working to relieve suffering and to bring the greatest joy to humankind.

In addition to strengthening the spiritual imperative to make peace, religions can contribute to human well-being in other ways—through the cultural flourishing they inspire and the traditions of learning, education, and truth-seeking they support. I hold the unchanging conviction that religion exists to serve humanity; humanity does not exist to serve religion. And it is by pursuing the challenge of serving humankind that religion can overcome the tendency toward fundamentalism and authoritarianism and provide the fertile soil from which a genuine culture of peace and empathy may grow.

It is my sincere hope that the publication of this book will encourage many dialogues, which will instill in people everywhere the courage to take on the "challenge of nonviolence" and the tenacity to work more creatively toward a just, peaceful, and humane world.

—*Daisaku Ikeda*
Founder, Boston Research Center for the 21st Century
President, Soka Gakkai International

INTRODUCTION

By Daniel L. Smith-Christopher

With the end of the global divisions created by the Cold War, we now confront the reality that new conflicts and tensions appear to threaten the human enterprise. Long simmering conflicts and hatreds boil over in regions where former Cold War *realpolitik* once enforced an uneasy truce or an artificial peace. As both individuals and groups struggle with the meaning of rapid socioeconomic change around the globe, it is hardly surprising that societies look back to cultural traditions and religious wisdom in order to strengthen their ability to look forward toward the third millennium. There appear to be comforts in an identification with an ethnic, national, or religious legacy that might serve as a solid mooring in rough seas of change and uncertainty (whether there are rational grounds for this hope or not). But in the late twentieth century, it is only too clear that these traditions can be manipulated and used to justify all kinds of violence, including the racist, xenophobic violence that seems determined to deny the integrity and the humanity of those outside the immediate group of interest—the "other" or the "foreigner" or the "heretic."

Such abuse seems particularly troubling in the case of religious-inspired violence and hatred. As moderns observe the role of religious enthusiasm in fueling conflict, it is all too easy to lay blame on the religious impulse itself as somehow inevitably divisive and destructive. I, along with the other writers of this text, submit that this is not so. I submit that the seeds of our very survival as a species find sustenance from these traditions of human response to the holy, to the sacred, to the sense of guidance and wisdom that we all too inadequately call the "religious impulse of humanity."

It is true that the seeds of war have found far too much nourishment in religious symbols, texts, and leaders. We deceive no one by simplistic notions that claim that "we all believe in peace." Clearly, we all do not. At least not so much that we would risk cutting off the war suppliers, shutting the arms factories, destroying the bombs, and declaring warfare itself an obsolete survival from less enlightened human origins.

Our call is a challenge with two edges: we direct our challenge to the traditions within which we participate with committed devotion, and we also challenge others from within our traditions—we challenge those who would seek to deny the very possibility of a way of nonviolence finding root in our respective religious traditions.

It is our goal to not only prove that nonviolence can be, and has been, supported from our respective (and collective) religious traditions, but that it is precisely the call to nonviolence that embodies one of the noblest values and sacred obligations of religion.

Peace is always and everywhere a challenge to live another way. In the spirit of this work, nonviolence is not an idea "imported" from outside our traditions, but is rather a call to central truths that drive us not away from our texts and sacred wisdom, but call us back to an encounter with the priceless treasures of our traditions.

NONVIOLENCE: WORKING ASSUMPTIONS

It is important to try to clarify the meaning of "nonviolence" at the outset. Nonviolence includes not only the refusal to engage in lethal activities but it also presumes a commitment to strive for conditions of fairness, justice, and respect in human relations. Nonviolence presumes a commitment to speak to the conditions that often give rise to warfare. Therefore, nonviolence is not centrally about the things one is opposed to, nor even about the actions one refuses to participate in. Nonviolence implies an active commitment to social change that would ultimately result in a fair distribution of world resources, a more creative and democratic cooperation between peoples, and a common pursuit of those social, scientific, medical, and political achievements that serve to enhance the human enterprise and prevent warfare.

Defining nonviolence always involves difficult debates of both a practical and a theoretical nature. There are many other activities in which individuals committed to nonviolence may choose to be engaged that go beyond such actions as the religious-based refusal to kill in settling disputes and an opposition to preparations for warfare. Different theorists and traditions have asked questions about the major strategies of social engagement—whether, for example, those committed to nonviolence can legitimately be involved in the destruction of property or forceful restraint of criminals within societies. These debates all presume active involvement in social problems by those committed to nonviolence. Obviously, there have been, and will be, varieties of opinion even within religious traditions—as shown by the different strategic approaches of Dr. Martin Luther King Jr., Mahatma Gandhi, Ustadh Mahmoud Taha—and among secular theorists of nonviolent strategy, including individuals like Gene Sharp. We see this book as an opportunity to further the dialogue on the spiritual content of nonviolent theory and practice.

Finally, we view this work as unfinished. This text is not intended to be a final statement but rather a thorough opening statement to provoke and inspire further thought as well as raise possibilities for discussion and new approaches to cooperative actions. In each case, the editors have asked the contributors to mention "frontiers" in their field of interest—questions that need to be pursued. If other scholars are inspired to take up some of these issues for serious research, then one objective of this work will be accomplished.

PEACE STUDIES, RELIGION, AND NONVIOLENCE

Warfare and social conflict at the end of the twentieth century are inseparable from issues of ethnic and religious identity. Religious thought has an important, if not central, role in many regions of conflict around the world. Christian Troll, in his study of Islam in India, writes:

> In the final analysis, the problems of Indian Islam do not differ essentially from those facing…all major religions—namely how to live as an important religious minority and in shared political responsibility with people of other faiths and ideologies. (Troll 1991, 246)

Similarly Haafkens writes of modern Africa, suggesting that "polarization along religious lines could seriously jeopardize the future of this part of the world" (Haafkens 1991, 300).

If religious values and symbolism are potential weapons (as well as essential to understanding a conflict), then surely the resources for reconciliation must also come from a more creative analysis of the religious cultural resources of the societies which are involved in the conflict itself. It is clear, then, that a major neglected element in the study of long-term and deep-seated conflict has been religious ideologies (with their collection of cultural symbols and signs) that are used by the warriors to encourage the great human and economic sacrifices of warfare (Mack 1983, 47-69). The very fact that emotional energy derived from such sources has been essential to conflict, however, reveals its significance for peacemaking.

In a profound sense, those of us for whom religious commitment is a meaningful center of our identity as human beings must take action on the basis of some kind of mutual program that would include statements like the following: We refuse to cede our faith traditions—our sacred writings and our prayers, our meditations and our acts of devotion—to the exclusive use, control, and interpretation by the warriors of history and their loyal apologists.

This book was initiated by the Boston Research Center for the 21st Century, which was founded in 1993 by Daisaku Ikeda, a Buddhist peace activist and president of Soka Gakkai International. The Center brings together scholars and activists in dialogue on common values across cultures and religions, seeking in this way to support an evolving global ethic for a peaceful twenty-first century. I wish to thank the Center for its vision and support. I am grateful to the Center's executive director Virginia Straus and to publications manager Amy Morgante for conceiving of this project. I am also grateful to Helen Marie Casey and Kali Saposnick for their strong and well-informed editorial support. I must accept responsibility for the editorial difficulties that remain in these texts, such as they may be. Whatever *successes* there may be, I would like to dedicate to the memory of two warriors of nonviolence, Steven S. Schwarzschild and John Howard Yoder.

It is the hope of the Boston Research Center and the authors of these chapters that we have, in some small way, contributed to the subversion of hatred and the undermining of those views and opinions that have fostered hatred.

Haafkens, Johann. "The Direction of Christian-Muslim Relations in Sub-Saharan Africa." In *Muslim-Christian Encounters,* ed. Yvonne Yazbeck Haddad and Wadi Zaidan Haddad, 300-313. Gainesville: University Press of Florida, 1995.

Mack, John. "Nationalism and the Self." In *Psychohistory Review*, vol. 2, no. 2-3 (Spring 1983), 47-69.

Troll, Christian W. "Sharing Islamically in the Pluralistic Nation-State of India: The Thinkers." In *Views of Some Contemporary Indian Muslim Leaders and Muslim-Christian Encounters,* ed. Yvonne Yazbeck Haddad and Wadi Zaidan Haddad, 245-262. Gainesville: University Press of Florida, 1995.

Chapter 1

JAINISM AND NONVIOLENCE

By Christopher Key Chapple

The Jain religion, currently practiced by approximately four million persons in India and several hundred thousand scattered across the globe, emphasizes the observance of nonviolence as its central teaching. The themes and practices of the Jain religious tradition extend backward into the early phases of Indian history. Above all else, nonviolence, care for animals, care for monks and nuns, and worldly renunciation characterize this important faith.

EARLY JAINISM

The earliest records of Indian religiosity can be found in the ruins and artifacts of the stone cities of the Indus Valley (*circa* 3500 B.C.E.) On various steatite seals, one finds depictions of animals being honored and adorned and meditating figures that indicate a proto-yoga tradition. It can be speculated that this proto-yoga tradition eventually gave rise to institutionalized monastic religious orders, including the Jainas, the Buddhists, the Ajivikas (who became extinct in the thirteenth century), and various sects of Yogis and Sadhus. These traditions, which emphasize renunciation of the world, involve embarking on a quest for liberation from all societal norms through the embrace of any one of a number of techniques for achieving spiritual ecstasy and liberation.

The *Rgveda*, the earliest of India's texts, describes the renouncers of India as follows:

The longhaired one carries within himself fire
and elixir and both heaven and earth.
To look at him is like seeing heavenly
brightness in its fullness.

CHRISTOPHER KEY CHAPPLE is professor of theological studies and director of Asian and Pacific studies at Loyola Marymount University in Los Angeles. Dr. Chapple has published several books, including *Nonviolence to Animals, Earth, and Self in Asian Traditions* (State University of New York Press, 1993). He recently convened a conference on Jainism and Ecology at Harvard University's Center for the Study of World Religions.

He is said to be light himself.
The ascetics, girdled with wind,
are clad in brownish dust (naked).
They follow the path of the wind
when the gods have entered them.
Wandering in the track of celestial nymphs and sylvan beast,
the longhaired one has knowledge of all things,
and with his ecstasy inspires all beings. (*Rgveda* 10.136)

The presence of the wandering, meditating ascetic has been part of India's landscape since the time of the Indus Valley Civilization. These proto yogis apparently held animals in high regard, as many images of meditators include groups of animals clustered around in seeming obeisance, and certainly without any fear of their human companion. Although we have no written source to confirm the attitudes toward animals in these portraitures, later texts of the Jain tradition attest to the primacy of a nonviolent ethic that looks benevolently on all beings.

By the time of historical Jainism (perhaps as early as 800 B.C.E.), *ahimsa,* or nonviolence, which includes not only abstention from physical harm to humans but also to animals, insects, and to a certain degree plants, becomes a hallmark of renouncer traditions. The earliest historical figure associated with this early tradition, Parsvanatha, taught a doctrine of harmlessness, or *ahimsa,* building on earlier practices. As a *Sramana,* or renouncer, he advocated the protection of various forms of life and perhaps advanced the systematized observance of religious vows that include nonviolence, truthfulness, not stealing, and nonpossession. According to the *Kalpa Sutra,* Parsvanatha lived 30 years as a householder, attained *kevala,* or liberation, 83 days after renouncing the world, and taught for 70 years as a Kevalin, an enlightened being, gathering 16,000 male monastic followers, 38,000 nuns, and thousands of lay disciples. He conducted his work in northeast India, primarily around the city of Varanasi, or Banaras. During his lifetime, thousands reportedly attained perfection. In his one hundredth year, he ascended Mount Sammeta and fasted for one month; finally "stretching out his hands, he died, freed from all pains" (Jacobi 1884, 275).

Although these stories of Parsvanatha are somewhat shrouded in hagiography and exact confirmation of his dates is difficult, several features indicated in these tales persist in contemporary Jainism:

the predominance of women in religious orders, the keen adherence to vows of nonviolence, and the practice of fasting to death when the end is near.

The earliest textual material we have for the Jaina tradition is the first part of the *Acaranga Sutra*, recorded within several decades of the death of the twenty-fourth and last Tirthankara, Mahavira Vardhamana, also known as the Victor, the Jina, from which the word Jaina derives. This text dates from the fourth or fifth century B.C.E. (Dundas 1992, 20). Several passages attest to the Jaina commitment to nonviolence, providing the complete articulation of this cardinal principle of Sramanic religiosity in India:

> All breathing, existing, living, sentient creatures should not be slain, nor treated with violence, nor abused, nor tormented, nor driven away.
> This is the pure, unchangeable, eternal law. (I.4.1)

> Injurious activities inspired by self-interest lead to evil and darkness. This is what is called bondage, delusion, death, and hell. To do harm to others is to do harm to oneself.
> "You are the one whom you intend to kill!
> You are the one you intend to tyrannize over!"
> We corrupt ourselves as soon as we intend to corrupt others.
> We kill ourselves as soon as we intend to kill others. (I.5.5)

> With due consideration preaching the law of the mendicants,
> one should do no injury to one's self,
> nor to anybody else,
> nor to any of the four kinds of living beings.
> A great sage, neither injuring nor injured,
> becomes a shelter for all sorts of afflicted creatures,
> even as an island, which is never covered with water. (I.6.5.4)

> Knowing and renouncing severally and singly
> actions against living beings in the regions
> above, below, and on the surface,
> everywhere and in all ways—
> the wise one neither gives pain to these bodies,
> nor orders others to do so,
> nor assents to their doing so.
> We abhor those who give pain to these bodies
> (of the earth, of water, of fire, of air, of plants, of insects, of animals, of humans).
> Knowing this, a wise person should not cause
> any pain to any creatures. (I.7.1.5)

15
.
.
.
.

Each of these quotes attests to the centrality of avoidance of harm in the Jaina religion.

Stemming from this perception that harm to others injures oneself, the Jainas assiduously practiced vows to prevent such digressions. By the time of Mahavira (540 to 468 or 599 to 527 B.C.E.), five vows guided the lives of all observant Jainas: nonviolence (*ahimsa*), truthfulness (*satya*), not stealing (*asteya*), sexual restraint (*brahmacarya*), and nonpossession (*aparigraha*). These became universal among religious mendicants, appearing in slightly revised form in Buddhist monastic manuals and verbatim in Patanjali's *Yoga Sutras*.

PHILOSOPHICAL JAINISM

During the next major phase of Jaina, which occurred in the second century of the common era, the scholar Umasvati articulated a philosophy of nonviolence that describes a universe brimming with souls (*jiva*) weighted by karmic material (*dravya*), many of which hold the potential for freeing themselves from all karmic residue and attaining spiritual liberation. He laid the foundation for a theory of multiple karmic colors and a path of spiritual ascent through 14 stages, culminating in total freedom, or *kevala*. His theories of karma and rebirth provided both a physical and metaphysical underpinning to support the practice of nonviolence.

According to Umasvati's *Tattvartha Sutra*, countless beings (*jiva*) inhabit the universe, constantly changing and taking new shape due to the fettering presence of karma, described as sticky and colorful. The presence of karma impedes the soul on its quest for perfect solitude and liberation. By first accepting this view of reality and then carefully abiding by the five major vows (nonviolence, truthfulness, not stealing, sexual restraint, and nonpossession), the aspirant moves toward the ultimate goal of untrammeled spirituality. At the pinnacle of this achievement, all karmas disperse and the perfected one (*siddha*) dwells eternally in omniscient (*sarvajna*) solitude (*kevala*).

This framework outlined by Umasvati grows to include the articulation of 148 distinct karmic configurations or *prakrtis*, to be overcome through a successive progression through 14 stages of spiritual ascent or *gunasthanas* (Tatia 1994, 279-285). Success in this process rests in the careful observance of *ahimsa*, through which one gradually dispels all karmas. Although no Jaina has achieved this state of ayogi *kevala* for several hundred years, thousands of Jaina monks and nuns in India practice a lifestyle that seeks to restrict and eliminate all obstructive karma through the observance of monastic vows.

To illustrate the nature of karma, a traditional story narrates how the personality types are associated with each of the primary five colors (*lesya*) of karma:

> A hungry person with the most negative black *lesya* karma uproots and kills an entire tree to obtain a few mangoes. The person of blue karma fells the tree by chopping the trunk, again merely to gain a handful of fruits. Fraught with gray karma, a third person spares the trunk but cuts off the major limbs of the tree. The one with orangish-red karma carelessly and needlessly lops off several branches to reach the mangoes. The fifth, exhibiting white or virtuous karma, "merely picks up ripe fruit that has dropped to the foot of the tree." (J. Jaini 1916, 47)

This story inspires many Jains to work at developing daily practices that work at lightening the quality of one's karma. For instance, many Jains fast regularly, particularly toward the final third of their projected life span, in an attempt to guarantee a spiritually auspicious future birth.

MEDIEVAL AND CONTEMPORARY JAINISM

In the third stage of Jainism, scholars such as Haribhadra in the eighth century and Hemacandra in the twelfth century, along with many others, have grappled with the issue of how best to articulate Jaina philosophy and practice, particularly in light of the broader Indian culture and society (see Cort 1998). During this time and up to the present, the Jainas have been quite effective in preaching the doctrine of nonviolence and convincing many Hindus and some Muslims to minimize the harm they cause, particularly to animals.

In the practice of nonviolence, Jainas refrain from all meat or meat-based foods. They avoid silk, which requires the slaughter of innumerable silk worms in its production. They participate in occupations that minimize harm to animals and humans, such as accounting, law, and certain forms of manufacturing. They actively

17

seek to spare animals from slaughter or harm by buying animals from slaughterhouses for release and by maintaining extensive animal shelters.

Anthropologist Lawrence A. Babb describes nonviolence in the Jaina tradition as central to Jain identity. He also notes that this links Jainism to the asceticism practiced on a modified basis by the laypersons and in most advanced form by its monks and nuns: "It is clear that faithful adherence to Jainism's highest ethic, which is nonviolence, necessarily means a radical attenuation of interactions with the world and, in this sense, nonviolence and asceticism can be seen as two sides of the same coin" (Babb 1996, 9). He goes on to note that

> Ascetics drink only boiled water so as to avoid harming small forms of life that would otherwise be present. Their food must be carefully inspected to be sure that it is free of small creatures. They must avoid walking on ground where there might be growing things, and they do not bathe so as not to harm minute forms of water-borne life. An ascetic carries a small broom *(ogha)* with which to brush aside small forms of life before sitting or lying. He or she also carries a mouth-cloth *(muhpatti)* with which to protect small forms of life in the air from one's hot breath. They may not use fire. They may not fan themselves lest harm come to airborne life. Although they are permitted to sing (and do so during rituals), they are not permitted to clap or count rhythms on their knees because of the potential lethality of their percussions. They may not use any artificial means of conveyance. (56)

However, it must be kept in mind that not all Jainas take up the rigorous vows reserved for monks and nuns. The 35 rules of conduct for the lay community stipulate that Jains must not enter into occupations that result in the "wholesale destruction of life" (Sangave 1997, 165). Specifically, Jains may not be "butchers, fishermen, brewers, wine-merchants, or gun-makers," nor may they take up jobs that involve "great use of fire, cutting of trees or plants, castrating bullocks, clearing of jungles by employment of fire, drying up lakes, rivers, etc." (165). Although Jains in the southern part of India are largely agriculturists and in years past many served as generals and warriors, they occupy a vast array of employment niches. Sangave has noted that they are "moneylenders, bankers, jewelers, cloth-merchants, grocers, and industrialists [and in] the legal, engineering, medical, and teaching professions" as well as in various departments of the Central and State Governments of India (166).

Jainism largely focuses on personal discipline. Its emphasis on strict observances of the nonviolence ethic has caused the tradition to draw criticism as "extremist" throughout Indian history; many of the early converts to Buddhism were drawn to preaching of moderation and the Middle Path. Because of its emphasis on interiority and a rigorous applied ethical code, and because of its alliances with power particularly in the southern Indian state of Karnataka during the medieval period, it might be asserted that the nonviolent ethic of the Jain tradition holds little in common with the Western tradition of peace movements.

Whereas most Jain monks and nuns in history have been in a sense cloistered from worldly involvement by their vows, a few exceptional Jain leaders have worked to influence the broader sphere through announcing their religious commitment and seeking to change the views of others. One example is Jincandrasuri II (1541-1613), the fourth and last of the Dadagurus, leaders of the Khartar Gacch (a subdivision of the Svetambara sect) who gained great fame for their religiosity. He traveled to Lahore in 1591 where he greatly influenced the Mughal emperor Akbar the Great. Jinacandrasuri convinced Akbar to stop an infanticide planned after one of Akbar's sons fathered a daughter under inauspicious astrological influences; a Jaina ceremony was held to mitigate the situation. As noted by Babb, who has written extensively on the Dadaguru tradition,

> Because of Jinabhadrasuri's influence Akbar protected Jain places of pilgrimage and gave orders that the ceremonies and observances of Jains were not to be hindered. He also forbade the slaughter of animals for a period of one week per year. (Babb 1996, 124)

In addition to these recorded historical instances, several miracles attributed to Jinabhadrasuri continue to inspire Khartar Svetamabra Jains in north India.

A contemporary activist leader of Jainism, Acarya Tulsi (1914-1997) similarly challenges the notion that monks utterly disengage from worldly life. Acarya Tulsi was appointed head of the Svetambara Therapanthi sect in 1936 at the young age of 22. For 58 years he served as its preceptor and leader and took up the task of promulgating the Jain principle of nonviolence to a wide audience and brought Jainism into dialogue with some of the broader contemporary issues of environmental degradation and nuclear escalation. He relinquished the office of Acarya to Yuvacharya Mahapragya in 1994. Deeply concerned about the prolongation of the Second World War, he wrote a plea for peace in June 1945 in which he articulated nine rules or universal basic principles that provide an outline of how to apply nonviolent principles. When Mahatma Gandhi received a published version of the following list, he lamented that it had not been published sooner.

1. The principle of nonviolence should be widely propagated throughout the world. Strong dislike and hatred for violence should be aroused in the hearts of mankind. *"Life is as dear to others as to one's own self, and not death."* This lesson should be widely taught and made the very breath of everyone. That will be sowing the seeds of peace.

2. Anger, pride, deceitfulness and discontent are the root causes of all unrest. All dispute and discord in this world owe their origin to these four causes. Every effort should be made to minimize these in every human being.

3. Outlook of education should be changed. Material gain or worldly ascendancy should never be the theme of education, rather stress should be laid on the development of inner self. Efforts should be made to achieve this end by every State and by International Cooperation.

4. The basis of all future governments should be justice, equity and good conduct and they should not be for exploitation or for selfish interests.

5. The scientific discoveries for material gains should be discontinued. At least they should never be used for the purposes of war.

6. More and more propaganda should be undertaken to preach real universal fraternity instead of national solidarity. Every endeavor should be made to minimize economic and political rivalry. Nationalisation which encourages young people to clash with other states should never be preached.

7. The habit of hoarding more than is necessary should be curtailed. Mutual rivalry, jealousy and the temptation to usurp power from others should be reduced. There should be no attempt to usurp or encroach on others' land or property as this is the cause of all armed conflicts.

8. No kind of unjust and oppressive steps should be taken by any person, nation or state against the weak, the depressed or the colored or other particular castes or communities. Principles of justice, impartiality and humanity should be more and more developed and practiced by every person, nation and state.

9. No principle or religion should be propagated by use of ordinary force or armed force or undue influence, etc. Every thing is more easily understood by right type of education and honest preaching than by use of force. For preaching, any idea or faith, no kind of force or undue advantage should be taken and along with this all legitimate steps should be taken to protect religious truth. Religious freedom should be granted to every individual. (Kumar 1997, 42)

These principles continue to ring true more than 50 years after they were written; conflicts throughout the world today, including those in South Asia, can be interpreted as violations of one or more of these basic rules.

On March 2, 1949, Acharya Tulsi initiated a campaign of self correction that garnered attention throughout India. He issued a list of vows to be followed by all in order to promote nonviolence and peace. In light of the social problems made evident in the years surrounding the Second World War and in the context of an India newly liberated by the activism of Mahatma Gandhi, Vinobha Bhave, and others, these vows helped provide a code of conduct for universal application:

1. I will not willfully kill any innocent creature.
2. I will not attack anybody.
3. I will not take part in violent agitations or in any destructive activities.
4. I will believe in human unity.
5. I will practice religious toleration.
6. I will observe rectitude in business and general behavior.
7. I will set limits to the practice of acquisition.
8. I will not resort to unethical practices in elections.
9. I will not encourage socially evil customs.
10. I will lead a life free from addictions.
11. I will always be alert to the problem of keeping the environment pollution-free. (Kumar 1997, 71)

As he walked through India on several occasions, and as he prepared his own monks, nuns, and lay disciples to promulgate Jain teachings, Acharya Tulsi worked for the social uplift of India. He campaigned against the ostracism of widows, child marriages, and ostentatious funeral practices. He sought to heal the rift between North and South India in the 1960s. He sent many disciples to the Punjab during the 1970s and 1980s to help quell the rampant terrorism during the height of the Hindu-Sikh rift. During the stock market scandals of 1994, he worked to heal difficulties within the Indian Parliament (Kumar 1997, 33-36). He also lent support to various environmental initiatives, including the 1995 Ladnun Declaration for a Nonviolent World and Ecological Harmony through Spiritual Transformation. Recognized by Mahatma Gandhi, Jawharlal Nehru, Indira Gandhi, as well as such Indian Presidents as Sarvepalli Radhakrishnan, V. V. Giri, Fakruddin Ali Ahmed, and Gyani Zail Singh, Acharya Tulsi provided to the world a model of how commitment to nonviolence and the life of asceticism can have a positive effect on the world.

CONCLUSION

Jain nonviolence, while not necessarily opposed to social uplift, focuses most directly on one's own spirituality, emphasizing that the avoidance of harm propels one away from karmic negativity toward increasing states of purification. I do not want to suggest that we dismiss the Jain vision as eccentric, extreme, or irrelevant. Rather, I would like to suggest that the virtue theory of the Jainas might help us with the perpetual challenge of how to integrate a vision of harmony and peace with the realities of a world fraught with suffering.

One of the most appealing aspects of India's renouncer traditions (Jainism, Yoga, and Buddhism) can be found in their emphasis on karma theory and voluntarism. According to these systems, the world through which we move depends, in large part, upon our own interpretations and projections. Due to our own personal choices, we set our own course, whether by force of habit or through a process of careful reflection and self-determination. Karmic theory suggests that by probing into the causes of our behavior, change can be effected.

The changeful choice advocated by each of these traditions requires a framing of life within the constraints of the ethical principle of nonviolence. Violent activities, stemming from an objectification of others and a consequent desire to control others, must be stemmed and substituted with nonviolent behavior. This requires a willingness to enter into a commitment to adopt new modalities of thought and action.

From a Jaina perspective, in order for nonviolence to be integrated into one's personal and interpersonal life and into work environments, one needs to investigate ways in which to foster virtuous conduct, cooperation, and communication. In the process, one might need also to look at the broader world situation and be willing to take risks. These risks might entail an evaluation of leisure activities. Do I cause harm to myself or others in the interests I pursue? One might also need to evaluate the quantity of goods one consumes and how much garbage results. Furthermore, one might need to reflect on the effect food has on one's body, and the effect of food production on the wider environment.

As we enter into the twenty-first century, violence will continue to confront us. Some violence will occur in our communities throughout our nation, and between nations worldwide. Violence will assault us remotely through television or other forms of media. Violence will simmer within us at times of unexpected stress and at times when our boundaries feel threatened and we feel the need to confirm our position. Other forms of violence will erupt when the structures of propriety and society clash with the realities of difference: difference in culture, in economic status, and between competing groups and within groups. By cultivating a commitment to not harm others and a commitment to work at helping others, the Jains have effectively advanced the cause of peace and nonviolence through the application of nonviolent vows.

Jain nonviolence invites the people of the earth to live sparingly and compassionately. Jainism began with brave naked ascetics in India and developed over several centuries into a sophisticated philosophy and way of life. In the *Acaranga Sutra*, Mahavira advises his nuns and monks to "change their minds" about things; rather than seeing big trees as "fit for palaces, gates, houses, benches..., boats, buckets, stools, trays, ploughs, machines, wheels, seats, beds, cars, and sheds," they should speak of the trees as "noble, high and round, with many branches, beautiful and magnificent" (II.4.2.11-12). So also, with a different view, with a different eye, if educated in a nonviolent perspective, people might likewise change the way they see the world and construe the world and others.

BIBLIOGRAPHY

Anuvibha Reporter, vol. 3, no. 1 (October-December 1997).

Babb, Lawrence A. *Absent Lord: Ascetics and Kings in a Jain Ritual Culture.* Berkeley: University of California Press, 1996.

Chapple, Christopher Key. *Nonviolence to Animals, Earth, and Self in Asian Traditions.* Albany: State University of New York Press, 1993.

Cort, John E., ed. *Open Boundaries: Jain Communities and Cultures in Indian History.* Albany: State University of New York Press, 1998.

Dundas, Paul. *The Jains.* London: Routledge, 1992.

Griffith, Ralph T. H., trans. *The Hymns of the Rgveda.* Delhi: Motilal Banarsidass, 1973.

Jacobi, Hermann, trans. *Jaina Sutras: The Acaranga Sutra.* Oxford: Clarendon Press, 1884.

Jaini, Jagmanderlal. *The Outlines of Jainism.* Cambridge: Cambridge University Press, 1916.

Jaini, Padmanabh S. *The Jaina Path of Purification.* Berkeley: University of California Press, 1979.

Kumar, Muni Prashant, and Muni Lok Prakash 'Lokesh'. "Anuvrat Anushasta Saint Tulsi: A Glorious Life with a Purpose." In *Anuvibha Reporter*, vol. 3, no. 1 (October-December 1997): 33-36.

Sangave, Vilas A. *Jain Religion and Community.* 2nd ed. Long Beach: Long Beach Publications, 1997.

Tatia, Nathmal, trans. *That Which Is: The Tattvartha Sutra of Umasvati.* San Francisco: Harper Collins, 1994.

Tobias, Michael. *Life Force: The World of Jainism.* Berkeley: Asian Humanities Press, 1991.

Chapter 2

THE PEACE WHEEL: NONVIOLENT ACTIVISM IN THE BUDDHIST TRADITION

By Christopher S. Queen

The Buddhist tradition is often praised for its peace teachings and the exceptional record of nonviolence in Buddhist societies over 2,500 years. While these praises are justified, it is important to recognize that Buddhism's contribution lies not primarily in its commitment to peace, *per se*—most world religions are committed to "peace" in some fashion—but in the unique perspectives and techniques Buddhists have developed for achieving peace within and between individuals and groups. One should also note at the outset that violence has not been unknown in Buddhist societies. Wars have been fought to preserve Buddhist teachings and institutions, and Buddhist meditation and monastic discipline have been adapted to train armies to defend national interests and to conquer neighboring peoples.

Nevertheless, the Buddhist tradition offers rich resources for peacemaking and the cultivation of nonviolence. Among these are its founding manifesto, the Four Noble Truths (Pali *ariya sacca*),[1] offering relief from the causes of human suffering; its cardinal moral precept, to refrain from harming living beings (*ahimsa*); the practices of lovingkindness, compassion, sympathetic joy, and equanimity (*brahmaviharas*); the doctrines of selflessness (*anatta*), interdependence (*paticcasamuppada*), and non-dualism (*sunyata*); the paradigm of enlightened beings (*bodhisattvas*) who employ skillful de-

CHRISTOPHER S. QUEEN is lecturer on the study of religion and dean of students for continuing education in the Faculty of Arts and Sciences, Harvard University. He earned degrees in the history and philosophy of religion at Oberlin College, Union Theological Seminary, and Boston University. He is co-editor and author of *Engaged Buddhism: Buddhist Liberation Movements in Asia* (State University of New York Press, 1996), *American Buddhism: Methods and Findings in Recent Scholarship* (Curzon Press, 1998), and *Engaged Buddhism in the West* (Wisdom Publications, forthcoming). He is currently working on a book on B. R. Ambedkar (1891-1956) and the conversion of India's untouchables to Buddhism.

vices (*upaya*) to liberate others from suffering; and the image of the great "wheel-turners" (*cakravartin*) and moral leaders (*dhammaraja*) who conquer hearts and minds—not enemies and territories—by their exceptional wisdom and kindness.

These teachings have found ardent champions in every culture touched by the Buddhist *dharma* (Pali *dhamma,* "teaching," "truth," "path"), principally those of India and Sri Lanka, Southeast Asia, China, Tibet, Korea, and Japan. In the modern world, nonviolent struggles for human rights and social justice have found Buddhist supporters in Asia and the West, spawning a new "engaged" style of Buddhist activism. Perhaps most notably, the Nobel Peace Prize has twice been conferred on Buddhist leaders during the past decade for their tireless efforts to liberate their compatriots from totalitarian regimes: His Holiness the Dalai Lama of Tibet in 1989 and Aung San Suu Kyi of Burma in 1991.

In this chapter we shall see how the Buddha and Asoka, Buddhism's greatest king, transformed the ancient Indian tradition of sacred warfare (symbolized by the chariot wheel) into a tradition of sacred peacemaking (symbolized by the "truth wheel" or *dharmacakra*). In the following sections, we shall examine the central teachings of Buddhist nonviolent peacemaking; historical challenges to the Peace Wheel tradition; the rise of socially engaged Buddhism; and two twentieth-century practitioners of Buddhist nonviolent activism.

TWO CHARIOTS IN ANCIENT INDIA

In the legend of the Buddha's life, a sage predicts that the young prince, Siddhartha Gautama, will become a "wheel-turner" (*cakravartin*) in the Vedic tradition of Aryan princes. The symbolism of the *cakra* ("wheel") recalled, for the prince's contemporaries in the Himalayan foothills of Northeast India in the sixth century B.C.E., the sun-disk of the sky-god Vishnu and the chariot wheels of a universal conqueror or "wheel-turner." Indra, lord of the gods, was said to conquer the universe with his war chariot. "With the unassailable chariot-wheel, O Indra, thou has overthrown the 60,099 warriors of the Sushravas" (*Rigveda* I.53.9). Known as the "chariot-fighter," Indra mirrored on high the conquest of the Indian subcontinent by Indo-European charioteers at the dawn of the Iron Age.[2]

In the *Sutta Nipata*, one of the earliest collections of Buddhist verse, Sela, a Brahmin well-versed in Vedic hymns, on meeting the Buddha for the first time and noting that he has the 32 physical characteristics of a *cakravartin*, exclaims,

> You deserve to be a king, an emperor, the lord of chariots,
> whose conquests reach to the limits of the four seas, Lord of Jambu Grove [India].
> Warriors and wealthy kings are devoted to you;
> O Gotama, exercise your royal power as a king of kings, a chief of men!

> The Buddha replied: I am a king, O Sela, supreme king of the Teaching of Truth;
> [But] I turn the wheel by peaceful means—this wheel is irresistible.[3]

The Buddha declares himself a *Dhammaraja,* or King of Truth, rather than a Lord of War. And, he implies, in a contest between a Lord of War and a Prince of Peace, the latter will be victorious.[4]

Whether the composition of these verses preceded or followed the tradition's designation of the Buddha's first sermon as "Turning of the Wheel of the Law" (*dharma-chakra-pravartana*), the notion that the Buddha transformed an ancient symbol of military conquest into a metaphor of nonviolence—a Peace Wheel, for the purposes of our discussion—was well established by the appearance of the first Buddhist art and architecture in the third century B.C.E.

The most famous image in Indian art, found today on Indian currency, is the lion capital of a polished sandstone pillar that the Buddhist king Asoka Maurya (ruled 270-232 B.C.E.) erected at one of the northern borders of his vast realm.[5] As prominent as the pillar's four lions, broadcasting the king's "lion's roar" (*simha-nada*) to the four directions of the empire, was the many-spoked Peace Wheel that appears below each lion to identify Asoka's policy of *Dharma-Vijaya,* "conquest by righteousness."[6] Following years of bloody campaigns throughout India, Asoka suffered deep remorse for the loss of life he caused. Becoming a Buddhist convert, he proclaimed a new era in one of his many Rock Edicts,

> For many hundreds of years in the past, slaughter of animals, cruelty to living creatures, discourtesy to relatives, and disrespect for priests and ascetics have been increasing. But now...the sound of

war drums has become the call to Dharma, summoning the people to exhibitions of the chariots of the gods, elephants, fireworks, and other divine displays. [Now the] inculcation of Dharma has increased…abstention from killing animals and from cruelty to living beings, kindliness in human and family relations, respect for priests and ascetics, and obedience to mother and father and elders.[7]

In the Buddhist Asoka's India, the state's vast stockpile of war chariots is saved, with fireworks and elephants, for patriotic holiday parades in an era of prosperity and peace.

For centuries the radical shift in social values wrought by Buddha and Asoka—from violence to reconciliation—was symbolized in stone art and architecture, from the low-relief sculptures representing the Buddha himself as a Peace Wheel, revered by followers at *stupa* sites (giant reliquary mounds) at Sanchi and Bharhut (*circa* 100 B.C.E.), to the well-known Preaching Buddha (Gupta period, *circa* 475 C.E.), in which the sitting Buddha demonstrates the wheel-turning hand gesture (*dharma chakra pravartana mudra*), while the Peace Wheel is venerated by the Lord's disciples below. The presence of two deer identifies the scene as the Deer Park at Sarnath, site of the first sermon.[8]

In 1948, following India's independence from colonial rule, the ancient chariot wheel, now symbolizing the rule of law in a peaceful society, was placed on the national flag of India.

TURNING THE WHEEL OF PEACE: CORE TEACHINGS

"A study of early Buddhist literature reveals the fact that the concept of peace appears as the pivotal point in the Buddhist system of social ethics," wrote O. H. Wijesekera, an eminent Sri Lankan scholar.[9] The Pali word for "peace," santi (Skt. *shanti*), ordinarily refers to what we would call "inner peace" and what in Buddhist psychology is called *nibbana* (Skt. *nirvana*), the complete absence of craving, agitation, suffering, and aggression. While the notions of peace and nonviolence in Western cultures are generally identified with inter-group relations, Wijesekera observes, "in Buddhism and other Indian religions, the primary emphasis is on the *individual* aspect of peace, and its social consequences are held to follow only from the center of the individual's own psychology."[10]

When the Buddha turned the Dharma Wheel after his enlightenment under the Bodhi tree, he expounded the Four Noble Truths: that all life is unsettled by feelings of dissatisfaction and pain (*dukkha*); that the arising (*samudaya*) of this disease is caused by ignorance of life's impermanence and a constant craving for comfort and security; that it is possible to achieve the extinction (*nirodha*) of these mental factors and to find the peace of nirvana; and that the Eightfold Path (*magga*) to this goal includes right (efficacious) views, aspirations, actions, speech, livelihood, effort, mindfulness, and concentration.[11]

Taken alone, the Four Noble Truths address the emotional needs of individuals—for inner peace, freedom from suffering, and a true understanding of existence. But the means to this goal, particularly the "steps" of right action, speech, and livelihood on the Eightfold Path, point directly to the social dimension of relationships in community. For laypeople, the great majority of Buddhists, *right action* entails the pledge to observe the Five Precepts (*panca sila*): abstention from taking life, from taking what is not given, from sexual misconduct, from false speech, and from the use of intoxicants. Here the quest for inner peace begins with the solemn vow of *ahimsa*, i.e., to protect all sentient beings from harm and injury. As we saw in the case of Asoka, this includes animals as well as humans, and, significantly for the early Buddhist community of monks (*bhikkhu sangha*), the abstention from killing animals in the ritual sacrifices of the Vedic religion. Indeed, the only religious "sacrifice" that the Buddha recommended to the Brahmin Kutadanta was the practice of the ethical Precepts themselves.[12]

In the ancient world no less than today, the practice of noninjury to others involved a complex calculus of intention and result. For example, not only was meat a dietary staple in most Buddhist countries, but the need for self-defense, law enforcement, national defense, and even agriculture (as the Jain followers of Mahavira, Buddha's contemporary, were quick to point out) inevitably involved some harm to living beings. One element in the Buddhist approach was to practice the Middle Way of moderation, avoiding professions involving killing (hunting, butchering, military service), i.e., practicing "right livelihood," on the one hand, and the Jain extreme of protecting insects by wearing a mask and sweeping the ground ahead when walking, on the other. Another element in the Buddhist approach to nonharming was to stress the *intention* or state of mind of the actor: monks could accept meat in their begging bowls as long as animals were not hunted or slaughtered expressly to feed them; similarly, a layperson might unintentionally harm another, say, in a household accident, without incurring the bad karma associated with premeditated assault or homicide.[13]

The most significant contributions of early Buddhism to the practice of nonviolence, I would suggest, are its techniques to counter the three evil roots (*hetu*) of action—hatred, greed, and delusion (*dosa, lobha, moha*)—the seeds of violence itself.[14] Here we learn that each of these reactions has its antidote: lovingkindness (*metta*) to counter hatred, generosity (*dana*) to counter greed, and wisdom (*panna*) to counter delusion. While it may be argued that greed and delusion are equal partners with hatred in the instigation of violence, it is irrational anger and hatred toward other individuals and groups that most often fuels the flare-up of violence and mayhem.

Accordingly, it is *lovingkindness meditation* (*metta bhavana*), cultivating goodwill toward oneself and others, that may be called the root practice in Buddhist nonviolence.[15] As the first exercise in a series of trainings called the "Divine Abodes" (*brahma vihara*), lovingkindness is complemented by the practices of compassion (*karuna*, sympathy for those in pain), joy (*mudita*, appreciating the good fortune of others), and equanimity (*upekkha*, maintaining impartiality in times of gain and loss). To meditate on lovingkindness, the practitioner begins by directing loving attention to his or her own state of being, repeating the formula in Pali or in one's own language:

Aham avero homi	May I be free from enmity
Abbyapajjho homi	May I be free from ill will
Anigho homi	May I be free from distress
Sukhi attanam pariharami	May I keep myself happy.

In a fashion similar to Christians' endeavor to love others as oneself, the Buddhist then extends the wish for freedom from enmity, ill will, and distress, and for happiness step-by-step to others—a beloved teacher or parent, a dear friend, a neutral or unknown person, and finally to a repellent or hostile person. "As one does this, one's mind becomes malleable in each case before passing on to the next."[16] Similar meditative training is recommended for the cultivation of compassion, joy, and equanimity.

The Buddhist approach to nonviolence, then, is grounded in a systematic "attitude adjustment" in which negative, reactive states such as hatred, greed, and delusion are transformed into positive social orientations through meditative self-training. But this reorientation to inner and outer peace entails other steps on the Eightfold Path: *right views* that establish a conceptual framework for meditative and ethical practice, *right aspiration* and *right effort* that motivate and sustain the practice; *right mindfulness,* by which the new attitudes are applied to situations and relationships in moment-to-moment living; and *right concentration,* by which the practitioner moves from merely "performing peace," as it were, to what the Vietnamese Zen Master Thich Nhat Hanh calls "being peace"—involuntarily exemplifying the enlightened mind of *nirvana.*[17]

While it is not possible here to treat all of the teachings of the Peace Wheel tradition, let us turn briefly to the conceptual world of Buddhist morality and then to the Bodhisattva's Path of universal liberation.

BUDDHIST PEACEWORK IN THEORY AND PRACTICE

The teachings of *karma*, moral causation, and *samsara*, the cycles of rebirth that encompass humans, animals, deities, and the damned, have formed the symbolic universe of many Asian cultures through the ages. In the Buddhist version, the human realm is superior even to the divine in that only a man or woman may cultivate the moral qualities that lead to Buddhahood and the final release from cyclic existence. Because moral causation is deeply individual—each person reaps his or her own rewards and punishments—and because the penalties for unwholesome reactions such as anger and violence are extreme—rebirth as a tormented being in one of the hell realms—the incentives to ethical behavior have always been great in Buddhist societies. But rather than cutting individuals off from one another, the notion of a circle of life connects all beings. Every being was once your own mother and thus deserving of respect, many believe, and the dangers posed by tormented beings offer opportunities for merit-making:

> Malicious spirits were not to be appeased with sacrifice but rather tamed through the power and goodwill of the holy individual. The theme of the human sage using superior mental powers to convert ogres came to typify in later centuries the way in which Buddhism interacted with the spirit cults it encountered in every land to which it spread. As for the benign spirits, the early texts treat their foibles with a gentle humor entirely devoid of awe.[18]

Needless to say, these habits of respect and goodwill could be anticipated at the purely human level as well, as Buddhist missionaries carried the Dharma throughout Asia.

But here is a paradox in the Buddhist view of liberation, for ultimately there are no "selves" to be respected, saved, reborn, or perfected in Buddhahood. Indeed, the teaching of *no-self* or *selflessness* (Pali *anatta,* Skt. *anatman*) lies at the heart of Buddhist psychology and ethics. As a corollary of the teaching that all phenomenal existence is impermanent (*anicca*), the doctrine of "no-self" affirms the conditioned, composite, and unstable nature of personality and explains why any effort to grasp or hold onto a permanent identity leads to disappointment, frustration, or even violence. Acceptance of this teaching, on the other hand, denies nourishment to the evil roots of action: How can one hate other "non-selfs"? How can one approach them with greed and grasping? How can one suffer in delusion when the truth of human nature is realized?[19] The result of this way of thinking is a more fluid and open-ended approach to others and to situations, suggesting multiple solutions to human problems and a reduction of the likelihood of conflict.

Another teaching that has supported the ethics of nonviolence in Asian Buddhism is that of dependent origination (Pali *paticcasamuppada*), the interdependence of all actions and beings in the cycle of rebirth, and thus the profound interconnectedness of the moral universe. While this psycho-cosmic conception—called the central insight of the Buddha's enlightenment—is related to the notions of selflessness and rebirth, it was developed in later Buddhist philosophy in the teaching of emptiness (Skt. *sunyata*), the deep interactivity and non-dualism of existence, in which each entity or person derives his, her, or its qualities from relationships—

and not a fixed essence, identity, or "own-being." Indra's Net, the metaphor of a web of jewels in which the facets of each reflect all of the others in the net, is another way of expressing the interdependence of all beings. The ethical implications of these doctrines have been obvious to Buddhists through the ages: realization of the impermanence and interdependence of selves in society and nature entails the deepest respect for all. To tear the fabric of this sacred relativity through violence entails dire consequences.[20]

As the Dharma ripened in India and was carried to neighboring cultures of Central, East, and Southeast Asia, new peace teachings evolved. Perhaps the most dramatic feature of the reform movement that came to be called the *Mahayana* (the "great" or "universal" vehicle) was the heroic activism of the bodhisattvas. The term bodhisattva ("a being, *sattva*, destined for enlightenment, *bodhi*") had always meant a future buddha. In the popular *Jataka Tales* of Shakyamuni Buddha's previous lives (357 as a human, 66 as a god, and 123 as an animal), the bodhisattva often sacrificed his or her life so that others might live. But in Mahayana teaching, where the possibility of limitless buddhas arose with the belief that *everyone has the potential to become a buddha,* myriad bodhisattvas appeared—disguised as the clever layman next door, for example (*Vimalakirtinirdesa Sutra*), as a kind of Superman or guardian angel who swoops down to save people from fires and floods (as in the *Prajnaparamita* or Perfection of Wisdom literature), as one who uses artful devices (*upaya kausalya*) to bring deluded or resistant people to the Buddhist path (as in the *Saddharmapundarika* or *Lotus Sutra*), or as one who protects mothers, children, and helpless members of society (as does the gentle *Kuan Yin* or *Kannon* of China and Japan).

These Buddhist saints, saviors, or "messiahs" (as one scholar has called them) have one thing in common: each has made a vow to postpone his or her own *nirvana* and remain in *samsara* long enough to save all beings from harm and bring them to enlightenment. Such an ideal, which combines the zeal of the barnstorming evangelist with the resourcefulness and patience of the social worker, may rightly be taken as a paradigm for the Buddhist peacemaker activists of today.[21]

Finally, the feature that places Mahayana Buddhism most squarely in the Peace Wheel tradition of Buddha and Asoka is its universalism (the *maha* in Mahayana), its promise of liberation to all people, but particularly to persons considered less qualified by society at large. As a harbinger of human rights thinking today, the *Lotus Sutra* presents the cases of Devadatta, the Buddha's evil cousin, and the Dragon King's precocious daughter, both of whom are revealed to be worthy of the highest spiritual attainment. In the case of Devadatta, who had been condemned to the hell realms for trying to kill the Buddha and stirring up discord among the monks, the Buddha predicts full redemption and Buddhahood. The Dragon Girl, barely turned eight, demonstrates her profound mastery of the Dharma and her own perfect Buddhahood before a cosmic assembly of enlightened beings and disciples. Just as the Buddha admitted untouchables, women, and a serial killer to his religious order, and just as Asoka extended his vast welfare system to the poor, the sick and elderly, criminals, animals, and forests, so the bodhisattva ideal of Mahayana Buddhism was extended across boundaries of gender, ordination, and social class.[22] Commenting on the universalism of the *Lotus Sutra*, Burton Watson concludes, "We learn that even the most depraved of persons can hope for salvation…in a realm transcending all petty distinctions of sex or species, instant or eon."[23]

CHALLENGES TO BUDDHIST NONVIOLENCE

As a practical ideology of nonviolence and universal humanism, Buddhism has made inestimable contributions to the diverse cultures of Asia. In Sri Lanka and Southeast Asia where *Theravada* ("elder-teaching") Buddhism took root, the daily appearance of monks on begging rounds served to exemplify the ideals of kindness and equanimity throughout the lay population. In the Tibetan cultural area, where as many as one-third of the able-bodied men entered monastic vocations, the quiet life of contemplation and service was revered as the acme of human achievement. In China, Korea, and Japan, Buddhism brought with it the moral cosmology of karma and rebirth and a pantheon of heavenly buddhas and bodhisattvas committed to the liberation of suffering humanity. At the popular level in all of these societies, the Buddhist teachings of non-injury, compassion, generosity, and selflessness have leavened the natural human tendencies of tribalism, territoriality, avarice, and violence.

But Buddhism became more than a source of popular piety and morality in its peregrination through Asia. The Peace Wheel tradition we have sketched became a mainstay of royal ideology—a powerful and pervasive civil religion, according to Donald K. Swearer. Following the paradigmatic reign of Asoka Maurya,

> Royal patronage of the Buddhist monastic order was reciprocated by institutional loyalty and the construction of religious cosmologies and mythologies that valorized the king as propagator of the Buddha's religion (*sasana*) and as the key to the peaceful harmony and well-being of the universe.[24]

Buddhist kings in ancient Ceylon, Thailand, Burma, and Cambodia, for example, were expected to embody the "ten royal virtues" (*dasarajadhamma*) of generosity, moral virtue, self-sacrifice, kindness, self-control, non-anger, nonviolence, patience, and righteousness. But they were also expected to keep social order and to regulate the claims of competing parties in the struggle for existence.

In the creation story of the *Aggañña Suttanta,* warring parties elect history's first king when social chaos breaks out over land and food. Such a king must be handsome, capable, and entitled to collect taxes to support the throne; but equally important, he must be one who is "wrathful when indignation is right, who should censure that which should be censured and should banish him who deserves to be banished." In a word, the Buddhist king must be prepared to use force to bring discipline and order to society.[25]

Here we encounter the paradox of the Peace Wheel in Buddhist history and the source of periodic challenges to the tradition of nonviolent social change. For with the evolution of a Buddhist civil religion, with its vesting of temporal power in the person of the *Dhammaraja* ("righteous ruler") and ultimately of the nation-state, a new bifurcation of powers came to be called *the two wheels of dhamma.* As S. J. Tambiah observes:

> [Buddhism is] a totality that includes the relation between *bhikkhu* and king (who encompasses and includes the householders), between the Buddha and Cakkavatti (Chakravartin) as the two wheels of the dhamma, between the sangha and the polity and society in

which it is located, between this-worldly and other-worldly pursuits. It is this totality that also makes Buddhism a world religion and not merely the pursuit of a few virtuosi.[26]

The Buddha and Asoka had transformed the ancient symbolism of the war-chariot wheel into an emblem of peace that had both religious and socio-political dimensions. For the Buddha this move involved his renunciation of the throne to become a spiritual teacher; for Asoka it involved the renunciation of military violence as the primary instrument of social control. But with the emergence of the Buddhist state as a dominant force in Asian history, the tradition of nonviolent sovereignty was, on notorious occasions, ignored or forgotten. Let us consider three examples.

In the *Mahavamsa* or Great Chronicle of Sri Lanka, King Dutthagamani (ruled 101-77 B.C.E.) experienced deep remorse after his bloody defeat of the Hindu Tamils. But unlike the parallel story of his Indian predecessor Asoka, Dutthagamani fought not only to unify his island kingdom, but also to defend the Buddhist way of life. His enemies were not only armed aliens with ties to the mainland, *they were Hindus, the worshipers of alien gods.* And unlike Asoka, the Sinhalese king was comforted by eight Buddhist monks who assured him that, in spite of the thousands slain in the battle, "only one and a half humans perished"—one who had pledged allegiance to the Buddha, the Dharma, and the Sangha (the "three refuges" of Buddhism), and another who had vowed to follow the Buddhist precepts. All the other Hindu Tamils were "unbelievers and men of evil life"—subhuman and deserving of death.[27] One sees in this example the way in which ancient religious hostilities overwhelm the peace teachings of each tradition in the conflict (note that Hinduism shares the Buddhist reverence for life, *ahimsa*); and religious, no less than political, leaders fuel the fires of bigotry and hatred. Surely Jewish, Christian, and Muslim militants in the Middle East, and Protestants and Catholics of Ireland, hold no monopoly on religious intolerance and holy war.

Similar examples of the compromise of the Peace Wheel tradition may be drawn from the history of Buddhist kingdoms in Southeast Asia, as Trevor Ling has done in *Buddhism, Imperialism, and War* (1979). According to Ling, "Buddhism in Southeast Asia has been successfully employed to reinforce the policies and interests of national rulers, often in their competition with one another for resources or prestige." The author chronicles the history of military violence within and between the Buddhist states of Thailand and Burma, as well as the efforts of civil and clerical officials to formulate the notion of Buddhist "holy warfare." A dramatic example is the speech delivered by the Thai Buddhist Patriarch (highest-ranking monk) on the occasion of the coronation of King Rama VI in the year 1910. The patriarch praised the new king as one ready to sacrifice his life for religion and country, thus setting the highest example of righteousness for all citizens. He said that the new king would bring prosperity to the Buddhist sangha and the kingdom of Thailand by directing the affairs of state with efficiency. Finally, he praised the king for steps he had already taken to prepare for war in times of peace: strengthening the army and navy, founding the Corps of Wild Tigers (an elite tactical force), and starting "the Boy Scout Movement to foster in boys the warrior spirit." In the printed version of his sermon, the Patriarch disputed the view that the Buddha ruled out "all wars and people whose business it was to wage war." Rather, the Buddha had condemned only "militarism . . . an intolerant and unreasoning hatred, vengeance and savagery which causes men to kill from sheer blood-lust."[28]

A third example of the subversion of the Peace Wheel tradition may be found in the near-universal support by Buddhist institutions and leaders for Japan's military excursions in the Sino-Japanese war of 1894-95 and the Russo-Japanese War of 1904-5; for the rise of militantly nationalistic "imperial-way Buddhism" (*kodo Bukkyo*) during the years 1913-1930; and particularly during the Pacific War against Japan's East Asian neighbors and the United States in World War II. In a sobering study, *Zen at War* (1997), Brian A. Victoria shows how the major Japanese Buddhist lineages lined up to demonstrate lock-step patriotism in the decades following the ascendancy of Emperor Meiji in 1868. In decreeing that "all absurd usages of the old regime shall be abolished and all measures conducted in conformity with the righteous way of heaven and earth," the young emperor had sought to disestablish a moribund and corrupt Buddhism in favor of the traditional state cult of Shinto. But by the first decade of the twentieth century, after Japan's bloody victories over China and Russia, Buddhist clergy and intel-

lectuals had already aligned their spiritual tradition with the medieval "way of the warrior" (*bushido*) and with the prowess of the
Japanese war machine. Here is the best-known Buddhist missionary to the West, D. T. Suzuki, in his first English-language publication on Zen Buddhism, for the *Journal of the Pali Text Society*:

> The calmness and even joyfulness of heart at the moment of death
> which is conspicuously observable in the Japanese, the intrepidity
> which is generally shown by the Japanese soldiers in the face of an
> overwhelming enemy; and the fairness of play to an opponent, so
> strongly taught by Bushido—all these come from the spirit of the
> Zen training, and not from any such blind, fatalistic conception as
> is sometimes thought to be a trait peculiar to Orientals.[29]

By war's end, Zen temples were sponsoring meditation training
camps for the armed forces, raising money for the purchase of new
aircraft (e.g., *Soto I* and *Soto II),* and recruiting middle school boys
to fly *kamikaze* ("divine wind") missions for the love of the emperor and in service to the Buddha. Alluding to a famous metaphor
in Zen training, Victoria concludes that for these boys, in search of
adventure and sacrifice, "Truly may it be said that their lives were
now 'as light as goose feathers.'"[30]

THE DAWN OF ENGAGED BUDDHISM

Over time, the symbol of the turning wheel in Buddhism
came to mean not only the exposition of the Buddha's enlightenment in skillful teachings and trainings, and the pacification of
human hearts and societies by virtuous teachers and rulers, but also
the rise of new schools of thought (e.g., the *Madhyamika* and
Yogacara) and complexes of belief and practice (*Mahayana* and
Vajrayana).[31] While the acknowledgment of its own impermanence,
implicit in the wheel symbol, is, paradoxically, a perennial charac-
teristic of the Buddhist tradition, it may also be credited for the
openness and energy with which Buddhists have adapted to new
cultural and political realities.[32]

The global emergence of socially and politically engaged Buddhism over the past century may be regarded as the latest turning
of the Peace Wheel, and credited to the vigorous encounter of Buddhist values with those of the West.[33] The term *engaged Buddhism*
was coined during the 1960s by the Vietnamese Thien (Zen) mas-

ter, Thich Nhat Hanh, to describe the activism of a small group of monks and laity who opposed the violence committed by both sides in the American Indo-China War.[34] But unlike the ultra-nationalist Buddhists we have described in the preceding discussion, Thich Nhat Hanh and the Unified Buddhist Church did not side with any of the combatants in the struggle. Rather, their allegiance was to nonviolence and peace itself. They attempted to "call the attention of the world to the suffering endured by the Vietnamese" by placing their own bodies in the midst of the conflict. This took the forms of walking between the battle lines in an effort to stop the bullets, for example, and of immolating themselves in gasoline fires on the streets of Saigon, as broadcast in the famous wirephoto of the Venerable Thich Quang Duc in 1963.[35]

By the 1990s engaged Buddhism was associated with a vast array of activities both within and outside of the international peace movement: in the struggle of the Tibetan people for self-determination and survival after 40 years of the Chinese occupation; the struggle of the Burmese and Cambodian peoples for human rights and democratic institutions; the rural development programs of the Sarvodaya Sramadana movement in Sri Lanka and the Asian Cultural Forum for Development in Thailand; the struggles for human rights of India's *Dalit* ("oppressed") or ex-untouchable populations, many of whom are converts to Buddhism; and the peaceful activism of three organizations inspired by the Nichiren tradition of Japanese Buddhism: the Rissho Kosei-kai, the Nippansan Myohoji, and the Soka Gakkai.

Engaged Buddhist leaders such as Tibet's Dalai Lama and Aung San Suu Kyi (leader of the Burmese opposition) have been awarded the Nobel Peace Prize for their struggles, while many others, such as Thich Nhat Hanh, Dr. A. T. Ariyaratna of Sri Lanka, Sulak Sivaraksa of Thailand, and Nikkyo Nawano and Daisaku Ikeda of Japan, have received international recognition for their tireless campaigns for social and political change.

In the West, engaged Buddhism has taken such forms as the Buddhist Peace Fellowship in Berkeley, California, founded in 1979; the urban social service programs of Soto Master Bernard Glassman and the Zen Peacemaker Order in Yonkers, New York; and the wilderness retreat and AIDS hospice programs sponsored by Dr. Joan Halifax and the Upaya Foundation in Santa Fe, New Mexico. Environmental and anti-nuclear activism, prison education and meditation programs, and lobbying initiatives on behalf of human rights and economic justice campaigns at home and abroad are only a few of the activities of Buddhist activists in North America, the United Kingdom, countries of the European Union, South Africa, and Australia.[36]

Engaged Buddhists have brought new beliefs and practices to the Peace Wheel tradition. Unlike followers of dharma in the past, who accepted the traditional Buddhist *theodicy*—the belief that suffering is caused by the ignorance and cravings of the sufferers themselves, and that one may overcome suffering and achieve *nirvana* only through individual effort—many engaged Buddhists have come to believe that much suffering in the world, particularly of the kind related to poverty, injustice, and war, is caused by the ignorance, cravings, and cruelty of persons other than the sufferer. Further, most contemporary Buddhists do not practice nonviolence, generosity, lovingkindness, and selflessness *in order to transcend this world* (i.e., to avoid rebirth in the future) or to help others to transcend the world. They practice out of the sense that their *deep relatedness* to others—as fellow beings on a planet or within an ecosystem, for example—obligates them to try to relieve that suffering, and that the net effect of such efforts will be a better world for all beings, human, animal, and vegetable. Finally, most engaged Buddhists believe in the efficacy of *collective practice* of the dharma, that is, in confronting the institutional abuses of negligent or oppressive governments and multinational corporations by such collective means as peace marches, rallies, demonstrations, boycotts, letter-writing campaigns, "base communities" for social action, and non-governmental organizations that publicize human suffering and work to overcome it.[37]

The inner-worldly (as opposed to other-worldly) orientation of engaged Buddhism is also reflected in the *egalitarian values* and non-hierarchical structure of its social organizations, which generally feature lay leadership and the equal participation and leadership of women. The *pragmatism* or activist bias of engaged Buddhism is accompanied by a de-emphasis on doctrinal orthodoxy that takes many forms: the *non-attachment to views* that Thich Nhat Hanh has called "the most important teaching of Buddhism" and placed at the head of the 14 precepts of his Order of Interbeing; and the *agnosticism* that Stephen Batchelor recommends for practitioners in *Buddhism without Beliefs*.[38] In both instances, there is a recognition that much of the violence in society and history has been sustained by a die-hard insistence on religious dogma, political ideology, and legal jurisdiction.

TWO EXEMPLARS OF ENGAGED BUDDHISM

As a way of bringing the new Buddhism into sharper focus— and of tracing its continuity with the ancient Peace Wheel tradition of nonviolent activism—let us look briefly at two of its most celebrated practitioners, B. R. Ambedkar (1891-1956), the Indian civil rights leader and Buddhist convert, and Daisaku Ikeda (b. 1928), the Japanese leader of an international lay Buddhist organization.

Bhimrao Ramji Ambedkar, the eighth of 14 children born to a Mahar family in one of the historically "untouchable" communities of Maharashtra in central India, was tutored by his father, a schoolmaster with the rank of major in the British Colonial Army.[39] Ambedkar's path to political and spiritual leadership was paved with an extraordinary education—capped by doctoral degrees from Columbia University and the London School of Economics, and a law degree from Grays Inn in London—and a meteoric career. Ambedkar pursued teaching and law school administration in Bombay, newspaper publishing, legal defense work for the growing civil rights movement on behalf of low-caste and untouchable citizens, service as representative to the Round Table talks in London that laid the groundwork for Indian independence, and leadership roles as cabinet minister and draftsman of the constitution for independent India in 1947. While raised as a Hindu, Ambedkar became deeply disillusioned over the seemingly unbreakable bond between Hinduism and caste discrimination. In 1935 he shocked India by declaring that he would seek a new religion that offered liberty, equality, and fraternity to the lowest members of society, and that he would "educate, agitate, and organize" until this spiritual revolution was complete.[40]

On October 14, 1956, during the twenty-five hundredth anniversary year of the Buddha's enlightenment, on the date traditionally associated with King Asoka's conversion, and in the central Indian city of Nagpur, associated with the preservation of the Buddhist Dharma, Dr. Ambedkar, his wife, and nearly one-half million untouchables embraced Buddhism. Six weeks later, Ambedkar died at the age of 65, and six months later his final work, the highly original *The Buddha and His Dhamma*, was published.[41]

In the writings and speeches of his final years, B. R. Ambedkar offered his followers a bold, engaged Buddhism directed to the relief of every kind of suffering—material, social, political, and spiritual. Even when advocating "agitation" for human rights, however, Ambedkar's Buddhism was unfailingly nonviolent, founded on his deep trust in the powers of moral suasion, collective protest, and constitutional law. Ambedkar's legacy—and his debt to the Peace Wheel tradition—may be seen today in the continuing struggle of the Dalit communities in India and abroad to find dignity and social justice, and in the revival of Buddhist practice in the land of its birth.

Daisaku Ikeda was born in Tokyo in 1928, the fifth of eight children in a family of seaweed farmers. As a teenager he lived through the devastation of World War II, which claimed the life of his eldest brother. In the years of poverty, ill-health, and social dislocation following the war, Ikeda sought the guidance of Josei Toda (1900-58), the second president of the Soka Gakkai, "Value Creation Society," a lay Buddhist organization whose activities are based on the Buddhist teachings of the thirteenth century reformer, Nichiren. Toda and the society's founder, Tsunesaburo Makiguchi (1871-1944), had been imprisoned in 1943 for refusing to support the war effort, an ordeal that contributed to Makiguchi's death. During the 1950s, Ikeda assisted Toda in building Soka Gakkai through vigorous recruitment of members throughout Japan. In 1960, Ikeda succeeded his mentor as president, and in 1975 he launched Soka Gakkai International (SGI) in recognition of the increasingly global character of the organization. Today SGI boasts more than 10 million members in Japan and some 1.3 million members in 127 other countries and territories worldwide.[42]

As SGI president, Daisaku Ikeda has channeled his tireless energies toward the support and reform of the United Nations as the world's premier peacemaking body; toward dialogues on peace and human rights with world leaders and thinkers, such as Nelson Mandela, Mikhail Gorbachev, Rosa Parks, Arnold Toynbee, and Linus Pauling; and toward educational and cultural projects such as the founding of the Soka Schools and Soka University, the Min-On Concert Association, and Tokyo Fuji Art Museum, all in Japan. In these activities, Ikeda has attempted to direct the wealth of Buddhist insight and practice to the relief of human suffering at the individual and collective levels:

> Global society today faces myriad, interlocking crises. These include the issues of war, environmental degradation, the North-South development gap, divisions among people based on differences of ethnicity, religion or language. The list is long and familiar, and the road to solutions may seem all too distant and daunting.
>
> It is my view, however, that the root of all of these problems is our collective failure to make the human being, human happiness, the consistent focus and goal in all fields of endeavor. The human being is the point to which we must return and from which we must depart anew. What is required is a human transformation—a human revolution.[43]

CONCLUSION

In this chapter we have explored some of the teachings and practices of the Peace Wheel tradition that date back to Gautama Buddha and Asoka Maurya. We have seen that, from the time of its earliest records, the Buddhist dharma has been directed to the achievement of inner peace and world peace through nonviolent means. Like other religious traditions, the successive turnings of the Peace Wheel in the Theravada, Mahayana, and contemporary engaged Buddhist movements have been rooted in the possibility of a life free of hatred, greed, and delusion. But, perhaps unlike other spiritual traditions, Buddhist nonviolent activism has been grounded in a practical curriculum of skillful actions appropriate for taming and transforming the mind, serving others in society, and affecting compassionate social change through collective action.

In facing history's report on the discord and warfare within Buddhist societies, we acknowledge that the Peace Chariot is only as reliable as its drivers and mechanics. On the other hand, Buddhists may take heart in the knowledge that their cherished vehicle of nonviolent peacemaking is still running, carrying new passengers, and bringing relief and joy to those who suffer.

RECOMMENDED READINGS

Himmalawa Saddhatissa. *Buddhist Ethics*. Boston: Wisdom Publications, 1997. A reliable introduction to basic teachings and practices in Theravada Buddhism.

Kenneth Kraft, ed. *Inner Peace, World Peace: Essays on Buddhism and Nonviolence.* Albany: State University of New York Press, 1992. A lively overview of the application of Buddhist teachings to a range of contemporary issues.

Christopher S. Queen and Sallie B. King, eds. *Engaged Buddhism: Buddhist Liberation Movements in Asia*. Albany: State University of New York Press, 1996. In-depth analysis of the rise and shape of the new Buddhism.

Thich Nhat Hanh. *Love in Action: Writings on Nonviolent Social Change*. Berkeley, CA: Parallax Press, 1993. Two decades of writings by an exemplar of engaged Buddhism.

Johan Galtung and Daisaku Ikeda. *Choose Peace*. London: Pluto Press, 1995. Dialogues between an activist and a scholar on the relationship between spirituality and history.

NOTES

[1] Buddhist words will be provided in Sanskrit or Pali, depending on context or familiarity to English readers. Sanskrit *dharma* will be preferred over Pali *dhamma* in most cases because of its familiarity. Likewise, the Sanskrit version of Buddha's name, *Siddhartha Gautama*, is more familiar than the Pali *Siddhattha Gotama.* Diacritical marks have been omitted.

[2] O. H. DeA. Wijesekera, "The Symbolism of the Wheel in the Cakravartin Concept," in *Buddhist and Vedic Studies* (Delhi: Motilal Banarsidass, 1994), 267-273.

[3] Sutta Nipata III.7.5-7. See *The Sutta-Nipata*, trans. H. Saddhatissa (London: Curzon Press, 1985), 65.

[4] The transformation of the war chariot to a peace chariot in ancient Buddhism makes an interesting counterpoint to the events in the Hindu poem, *Bhagavad Gita* (an episode in the Indian national war epic, *Mahabharata*). Here the protagonist, young general Arjuna, attempts to prevent a war from his place in the lead chariot, only to be reminded by his charioteer, the divine Lord Krishna, that his caste duty is to fight. See *The Bhagavad Gita: Krishna's Counsel in Time of War*, trans. Barbara Stoler Miller (Toronto: Bantam Books, 1986). The contrast between the two traditions is heightened by the fact that the historical Buddha and the legendary Arjuna are of the same caste, the *kshatriya* or military/administrative caste.

[5] For a thorough discussion of the relationship between Buddhist social ethics and the state, represented by the image of "the two wheels," see Gananath Obeyesekere, Frank Reynolds, and Bardwell Smith, ed., *The Two Wheels of Dhamma: Essays on the Theravada Tradition in India and Ceylon* (Chambersburg, Pa.: American Academy of Religion, 1972).

[6] See Robert E. Fisher, *Buddhist Art and Architecture* (London: Thames and Hudson, 1993), 20.

[7] From Rock Edict IV, in N. A. Nikam and Richard McKeon, ed. and trans., *The Edicts of Asoka* (Chicago: University of Chicago Press/Midway, 1978), 31.

[8] Fisher, 20-55. The ancient Buddhist ritual of circumambulation (*pradaksina*) of the *mandala-* or wheel-shaped Buddhist *stupa* while reciting, chanting, or singing the words of the liturgy may be regarded as a ritualized "turning of the wheel of the Dharma" accessible to both ordained and lay practitioners. See Sukumar Dutt, *The Buddha and Five After-Centuries* (London: Luzac, 1957), 163-178; and Govinda, *The Psycho-Cosmic Symbolism of the Buddhist Stupa* (Emeryville, Calif.: Dharma Publishing, 1976).

[9] O. H. DeA. Wijesekere, "The Concept of Peace as the Central Notion of Buddhist Social Psychology," in *Buddhist and Vedic Studies* (Delhi: Motilal Banarsidass, 1994), 94.

[10] Ibid.

[11] For a modern interpretation of the Four Noble Truths, see Walpola Rahula, *What the Buddha Taught* (New York: Grove Press, 1959), 16-50.

[12] See discussion in Hammalawa Saddhatissa, *Buddhist Ethics* (Boston: Wisdom Publications, 1997), 60.

[13] Ibid., 60f.

[14] These mental factors are perhaps more tellingly called *àsavas*, emotional "secretions."

[15] See Sharon Salzberg, *Lovingkindness: The Revolutionary Art of Happiness* (Boston: Shambhala Publications, 1997).

[16] Ibid., 62-64.

[17] See Thich Nhat Hanh, *Being Peace* (Berkeley: Parallax Press, 1987).

[18] Richard H. Robinson and Willard L. Johnson, *The Buddhist Religion: A Historical Introduction*, 4th ed. (Belmont, Calif.: Wadsworth, 1997), 22-23.

[19] For a profound discussion of this teaching in the Pali literature, see Steven Collins, *Selfless Persons: Imagery and Thought in Theravada Buddhism* (Cambridge: Cambridge University Press, 1982).

[20] See Joanna Macy, *Mutual Causality in Buddhism and General Systems Theory* (Albany: State University of New York Press, 1991); Frederick J. Streng, *Emptiness: A Study in Religious Meaning* (Nashville: Abingdon Press, 1967); Francis H. Cook, *Hua-yen Buddhism: The Jewel Net of Indra* (University Park: The Pennsylvania State University Press, 1977).

[21] See Har Dayal, *The Bodhisattva Doctrine in Buddhist Sanskrit Literature* (London: Kegan, Paul, Trench, Trubner, 1932); Leslie S. Kawamura, ed., *The Bodhisattva Doctrine in Buddhism* (Waterloo, Canada: Canadian Corporation for Studies in

Religion, 1981); Donald S. Lopez Jr. and Steven C. Rockefeller, ed., *The Christ and the Bodhisattva* (Albany: State University of New York Press, 1987).

[22] On Asoka's welfare policies, see Robert A. F. Thurman's succinct discussion in "Edicts of Asoka," in *The Path of Compassion,* ed. Fred Eppsteiner, 111-119.

[23] Burton Watson, trans., *The Lotus Sutra* (New York: Columbia University Press, 1993), xviii-xix. The episodes concerning Devadatta and the Dragon Girl occur in chapter 12, 182-189. This tendency in Mahayana thought was eventually expressed in the teachings of "universal Buddha-Nature" *(Tathagatagarbha)* and "original enlightenment" (Japanese *hongaku shiso*) in such schools as the Indian Yogacara, Chinese T'ien T'ai (Japanese Tendai), and the meditation or Ch'an/ Zen schools of East Asia. Some scholars have recently debated whether this direction in Buddhist thought was compatible with the spirit of the ancient Dharma, and whether it may support a social ethic based on human rights and nonviolence. See Jamie Hubbard and Paul L. Swanson, ed., *Pruning the Bodhi Tree: The Storm over Critical Buddhism* (Honolulu: University of Hawaii Press, 1997).

[24] Donald K. Swearer, *The Buddhist World of Southeast Asia* (Albany: State University of New York Press, 1995), 64.

[25] For the significance of the *Agganna Sutta* in Buddhist civil religion, see S. J. Tambiah, *World Conqueror and World Renouncer: A Study of Buddhism and Polity in Thailand against a Historical Background* (Cambridge: Cambridge University Press, 1976), 9-18. In this connection it is useful to compare the circumstances surrounding the debate over the anointment of Israel's first king in the Biblical narratives of I Samuel.

[26] Ibid., 15-16.

[27] *Mahavamsa* 25:101-111, cited by S. J. Tambiah, *Buddhism Betrayed: Religion, Politics, and Violence in Sri Lanka* (Chicago: University of Chicago Press, 1992), 1.

[28] Trevor Ling, *Buddhism, Imperialism, and War* (London: George Allen & Unwin, 1979), 136f.

[29] Quoted by Brian Victoria, *Zen at War* (New York: Weatherhill, 1997), 105.

[30] Ibid., 129.

[31] Robinson and Johnson, *The Buddhist Religion,* 33.

[32] I once asked a Burmese meditation master if the teaching of impermanence was not itself a "permanent truth" about reality. He smiled, fluttered his fan, and called on another student.

[33] For a discussion of the scope and history of engaged Buddhism, see Christopher S. Queen, "Introduction: Sources and Shapes of Engaged Buddhism," in *Engaged Buddhism: Buddhist Liberation Movements in Asia,* ed. Christopher S. Queen and Sallie B. King (Albany: State University of New York Press, 1996).

[34] "In the 1930s, the Buddhist scholars [in Vietnam] had already discussed the engagement of Buddhism in modern society and called it *Nhan Gian Phat Giao,* or engaged Buddhism," wrote Thich Nhat Hanh in *Vietnam: Lotus in a Sea of Fire* (New York: Hill and Wang, 1967), 42.

[35] See Thich Nhat Hanh, *Vietnam: Lotus in a Sea of Fire,* and *Love in Action: Writings on Nonviolent Social Change* (Berkeley: Parallax Press, 1993); Sallie B.

King, "Thich Nhat Hanh and the Unified Buddhist Church: Nondualism in Action," in Queen and King, *Engaged Buddhism*, 321-364.

[36] See Christopher S. Queen, ed., *Engaged Buddhism in the West* (Boston: Wisdom Publications, forthcoming).

[37] For examples of the burgeoning literature on engaged Buddhism in many of these areas, see Fred Eppsteiner, ed., *The Path of Compassion: Writings of Socially Engaged Buddhism* (Berkeley: Parallax Press, 1988); Kenneth Kraft, ed., *Inner Peace, World Peace: Essays on Buddhism and Nonviolence* (Albany: State University of New York Press, 1992); Joanna Macy, *World as Lover, World as Self* (Berkeley: Parallax Press, 1991); Allan Hunt Badiner, ed., *Dharma Gaia: A Harvest of Essays in Buddhism and Ecology* (Berkeley: Parallax Press, 1990). Parallax Press is the preeminent publisher of the writings of Thich Nhat Hanh and other engaged Buddhist authors, while the quarterly, *Turning Wheel: Journal of the Buddhist Peace Fellowship* (published in Berkeley since 1979) is the leading periodical of engaged Buddhism in North America.

[38] For a discussion of the theme of "Buddhist self-negation" among Buddhist activists, see Sallie B. King's concluding chapter in Queen and King, *Engaged Buddhism*, 422-430; for Stephen Batchelor's Buddhist agnosticism, see *Buddhism without Beliefs* (New York: Riverhead Books, 1997).

[39] See Sangharakshita, *Ambedkar and Buddhism* (Glasgow: Windhorse Publications, 1986) for a readable introduction; Dhananjay Keer, *Dr. Ambedkar: Life and Mission*, 3rd ed. (Bombay: Popular Prakashan, 1971) for a full biography; Christopher S. Queen, "Dr. Ambedkar and the Hermeneutics of Buddhist Liberation," in Queen and King, *Engaged Buddhism*, for a discussion of the Indian leader's place in Buddhist thought.

[40] Tellingly, both of Ambedkar's slogans were taken from human rights struggles he had studied in the West: the French Revolution ("liberté, equalité, fraternité") and the American labor movement ("Educate, Agitate, Organize").

[41] Ambedkar's collected works, *Dr. Babasaheb Ambedkar Writings and Speeches*, edited by Vasant Moon, are available in 15 volumes from the Education Department of the Government of Maharashtra, Bombay, 1987-1995.

[42] For a discussion of Soka Gakkai's history and contribution to the rise of engaged Buddhism, see Daniel A. Metraux, "The Soka Gakkai: Buddhism and the Creation of a Harmonious and Peaceful Society," in Queen and King, *Engaged Buddhism*, 365-400. Biographical details taken from "Daisaku Ikeda: A Profile," a pamphlet available from Soka Gakkai International, n.d.

[43] Daisaku Ikeda, "Thoughts on Education of Global Citizenship," delivered at Teachers College, Columbia University, June 13, 1996 (Tokyo: Soka Gakkai, 1996), 24-25. See also Ikeda's book-length dialogues with authorities on world peace: Aurelio Peccie (founder of the Club of Rome) and Daisaku Ikeda, *Before It is Too Late* (Tokyo: Kodansha International, 1984); Johan Galtung (founder of the International Peace Research Institute and professor of peace studies at the University of Hawaii) and Daisaku Ikeda, *Choose Peace* (London: Pluto Press, 1995).

Chapter 3

SUBVERTING HATRED: PEACE AND NON-VIOLENCE IN CONFUCIANISM AND DAOISM

By Tam Wai Lun

Both the Confucian and Daoist traditions began in the period of Warring States (403-221 B.C.E.). As a response to the hostile and chaotic situation of the warring period, both traditions condemned offensive war and discouraged the use of arms in the ordering of a state. Ironically, China was eventually unified under the Qin dynasty (221-206 B.C.E.) by warfare. Wars on the borders have remained a major concern throughout Chinese history.

This paper will argue that the ideal of peace and nonviolence taught in the Confucian and Daoist traditions was realized at a regional level in traditional Chinese society. Peacemaking was carried out by Chinese people at the grassroots level—people who read few or no written texts.

People at the grassroots level are related to the two elite traditions in two ways. Confucian values basically provide the framework of their kinship system, and their local religion is loosely connected with religious Daoism. Here we touch upon the complicated problem of the two terms, Confucianism and Daoism, which we must clarify before proceeding any further.

There has been a long tradition among scholars of trying to understand Chinese religion from the point of view of three teachings: Confucianism, Daoism, and Buddhism. Of the three, Buddhism is imported from India while Confucianism and Daoism are indigenous Chinese religions. Recent research, however, has shown that the threefold division for understanding Chinese religion is inadequate, as it represents mostly the ideas of well-educated elites

TAM WAI LUN is an assistant professor in the Department of Religion at the Chinese University of Hong Kong. He is undertaking a research project with Professor John Lagerwey on *Religious Festivals: Social Structure and Local Identity in Guangdong*. Close ethnographic descriptions of the chief festivals of eight counties in northern Guandong Province will be produced.

(Lopez 1996, 3ff). Another way of studying Chinese religion is to focus on those aspects of religious life that most Chinese people, especially the common people and the uneducated, share. Such aspects of Chinese religion are often described by a separate category: Chinese popular religion. This approach also reflects a recent trend in research in social science and humanities that is characterized by a general move away from studies of the elite (Teiser 1996, 25). It also involves an understanding of religion as not only a system of beliefs but also a system of rituals and practices.

THE ELITE AND THE FOLK CULTURE

Studying Chinese religion from the bottom up does not necessarily exclude the elite class. Most scholars believe in a two-way exchange between the cultures of the two tiers: the lower class and the elite (Redfield 1959, 86-87). Elements from the culture of the lower classes are often adopted by the elite, while the elite culture at times shapes the culture of the lower class. Common elements, therefore, can be found in both levels of culture. One example is found in the kinship system in China. Confucian ethics, an elite culture, informs the Chinese family system both on the elite and popular level. Confucian ethics is expressed in the form of lineage regulations and rules written in all lineage registers. These are passed on orally to the illiterate family members. Chinese on the folk level is, therefore, shaped by the Confucian teaching through their lineage and kinship system. Similarly, Daoism, and to a certain extent Buddhism, also informs religious life at the popular level. Not only the pantheon but also the forms of rituals from the elite religious systems are adopted by local ritual masters, also known as local Daoists.

The terms Confucianism and Daoism cover a broad range of phenomena (Teiser 1996, 5-6). Confucianism refers to the Five Classics that Confucius (551-479 B.C.E.) is believed to have edited, which were made the foundation of the official system of education and scholarship in 136 B.C.E. Confucianism also denotes a state-sponsored cult with complex rituals, a cult responsible for temples built throughout the Han empire in honor of Confucius. Finally, Confucianism includes a conceptual scheme synthesizing Confucius' ideas and various cosmologies popular long after him. Scholar Dong Zhongshi (ca. 179-104 B.C.E.) was instrumental in this synthesis.

As for the word Daoism, scholars usually divide it into two forms: philosophical Daoism and religious Daoism (Creel 1970, 11, 24). There are two texts associated with the former: (1) the *Daodejing* (a classic on the Way and Its Power), attributed to Laozi who lived during the sixth century B.C.E., and (2) the *Zhuangzi*, named for its author Zhuangzi (ca. 370-301 B.C.E.). Daoism also refers to religious movements that began to develop in the late second century C.E. Examples of some of these movements are the Celestial Master (*Tianshi Dao*) in the second century, the Great Purity (*Taiqing*) in the fourth century, the Highest Clarity (*Shanqing*) in the second half of the fourth century, Numinous Treasure (*Lingbao*) in the fifth century, and the Supreme Unity (*Tayi*) and complete Perfection (*Quanzhen*) in the twelfth century. Obviously, it is not possible to discuss all aspects covered by the two terms, Confucianism and Daoism, in one short essay. This paper will therefore seek to examine the themes of peace and nonviolence in Confucian and Daoist tradition as practiced on the folk level.

About 70 percent of the Chinese population still lives in villages despite recent widespread urbanization of the country (Lagerwey 1996, 2). An investigation of village life is, therefore, indispensable to any understanding of China, especially traditional China.

As we have pointed out, the elite culture and the folk culture are not unrelated. We will start our investigation from the elite level, although our focus will be on the popular level. As for the elite level, we will limit ourselves to the Confucian classic, *Analects,* and the Daoist classic, *Daodejing.* We will also include a brief discussion of Mozi (470-391 B.C.E.), a critic of Confucian ideas, who produced the earliest systematic essay in Chinese history arguing against warfare. These are the most important documents from the ancient Chinese written traditions that support the position of nonviolence.

Our discussion will first examine the themes of peace and nonviolence in the two classics. Second, we will investigate to what extent and in what ways the ideals of peace and nonviolence taught in the classics have penetrated to and are still carried out at the grassroots level in China. Again, we could not cover the whole of China in a short essay such as this. We, therefore, will concentrate on a recent field work study entitled, "The Structure and Dynamics of Chinese Rural Society in South China," conducted by John Lagerwey and other Chinese scholars. The project is an ongoing ethnographic study that covers three provinces in the South, namely, Fujian (south), Jiangxi (south), and Guangdong (north and east). Based on some of the findings of Lagerwey's project, we are seeking by personal interviews of old people to investigate how the Chinese in villages of South China manage to bring peace and avoid violence in their daily life—an ideal advocated in both the Confucian *Analects* and Daoist *Daodejing*.

When the Duke of Wei consulted Confucius about military formation, Confucius replied that he had never studied the matter of commanding troops (*Analects* 15:1). In reality, Confucius had discussed with his disciples whom he would take with him when he led the armed forces. This shows that he indeed was knowledgeable in military affairs but he was not willing to give advice on military matters.

In his discussion with his disciples about the minister Guanzhong, Confucius praised him for repeatedly helping Duke Huan to unite the feudal lords without the use of force (*Analects* 14:16). Confucius described Guanzhong as a man of benevolence—the supreme virtue in Confucius' teaching, although Guanzhong fell short of benevolence by serving Duke Huan who had his brother, Prince Jiu, killed. Apparently, according to Confucius, bringing peace among the states compensates for Guanzhong's serving an immoral king. We can see how Confucius emphasizes peacemaking.

When he discussed government with Zigong, Confucius commented that among the three necessary qualifications for good government, food, arms, and trust by the people, if one had to give up one of these three, one should give up arms (*Analects* 12:7). Not only does Confucius put a low priority on the use of military force, but also on the use of other forms of force in law enforcement like capital punishment (*Analects* 12:9). On the matter of the proper ordering of the state, Confucius teaches a return to virtue. He supports government by personal virtue. A virtuous ruler, according to Confucius, could lead his people by example and the model of his own goodness. Commenting on Confucius' ideas, Mencius observes,

> Confucius rejected those who enriched rulers not given to the practice of benevolent government. How much more would he reject

those who do their best to wage war on their behalf. In wars to gain land, the dead fill the plain; in wars to gain cities, the dead fill the cities…. Hence those skilled in war should suffer the most severe punishments (*Mencius,* Book IV, Part A, 14).

Mencius is right in claiming that Confucius discourages the use of arms in government, but we must add that Confucius did not reject war without qualification. When he heard that Chenheng killed his lord, Duke Jian of Qi, Confucius went in person to request Duke Ai of Lu to send an army to punish Chen (*Analects* 14:21). Confucius condemned the sending of untrained common people to war (*Analects* 13:30), but when they were properly trained for seven years, they should be ready to "take up arms" (*Analects* 13:29). Therefore, Confucius did not deny totally the role of arms in government. He taught that one should repay an injury with justice but repay a good turn with a good turn (*Analects* 14: 34). The use of arms cannot be totally avoided, but according to *Analects*, fasting, war, and sickness were the things over which Confucius exercised care. As the orthodox Confucian tradition advocates benevolent government, it rejects the way of a despot, or the way of force, in favor of the idea of a "kingly way" or the way of moral power (Chan 1963, 50). The idea of benevolent government in the Confucian tradition discourages the use of force and puts the Confucian tradition close to our modern idea of peace and nonviolence.

In the Daoist classic *Daodejing*, we find even stronger statements rejecting the use of force in government. In the *Daodejing*, Laozi states:

One who assists the ruler of men by means of the way does not intimidate the empire by a show of arms….
Where troops have encamped
There will brambles grow;
In the wake of a mighty army
Bad harvests follow without fail. (*Daodejing* 30:69)

The way of Daoism teaches simplicity, spontaneity, tranquillity, weakness, and non-action (*wuwei*), which means taking no action that is contrary to nature and letting nature takes its own course (Chan 1963, 136). Such a teaching naturally denies the use of force and violence. In chapter 31, Laozi continues:

It is because arms are instruments of ill omens and there are things that detest them that one who has the way does not abide by their use.... When one is compelled to use them, it is best to do so without relish. There is no glory in victory, and to glorify it despite this is to exult in the killing of men. One who exults in the killing of men will never have his way in the empire. (*Daodejing* 31:72)

Therefore, according to the *Daodejing*, the use of force and arms is a curse to the country. Although *Daodejing* does not totally rule out the use of force, Laozi claims that war is found only in the empire when the concepts of Daoism do not prevail (*Daodejing* 41).

The first systematic argument against warfare in China is advanced by Mozi who lived in the period of Warring States. Mozi is noted for his teachings of universal love for all humans. To begin with, Mozi was a student of Confucianism. Dissatisfied with Confucius' complicated teachings on decorum, Mozi became a critic of the Confucian tradition. His essay, "Against Offensive Warfare," is the first of its kind in Chinese history. In order to complete his self-assigned mission of "promoting what is beneficial to the world and to eliminate what is harmful" (Watson 1963, 39), Mozi and his followers worked actively in bringing peace and non-aggression among the states. He and his followers even risked their lives in assisting in the defense of a besieged state (Lowe 1992, 18).

Mozi's essay, "Against Offensive Warfare," consists of three parts: (1) Mozi first demonstrates by logical argument the unrighteousness of war. (2) He then details the wastefulness and economic unprofitability of wars of conquest. (3) Finally, Mozi points out that war benefits neither Heaven, nor spirits, nor human beings.

In demonstrating the unrighteousness of war, Mozi argues that the unrighteousness of an act is in proportion to the harm caused to others. Stealing horses and cattle is, therefore, worse than stealing chickens and pigs, which is, in turn, worse than stealing peaches and plums. The murder of one hundred men is worse than the murder of 10 and, in turn, the murder of 10 is worse than the murder of one. Mozi laments that people can readily recognize small acts of unrighteousness but fail to perceive great unrighteousness like war (Watson 1963, 50).

In pointing at war as unproductive and destructive, Mozi observed that in war the productivity of the state will be diminished and there will be a great loss in human resources and materials. According to Mozi's calculation, an army is composed of at least hundreds of nobles, thousands of commoners, and tens of thousands of laborers. A war takes months or years, during which production comes to a standstill. Only one-fifth of the equipment needed for war, such as chariots, horses, and tents, can be recovered after use. To subdue a small walled city of three to seven square miles involves the death of literally hundreds of thousands of people (Watson 1963, 54-55). A successful invasion gains only a small amount of land. Mozi concludes that for a successful invasion, gains *are less than losses* since one gains what is in surplus, land, but loses what is insufficient, human resources.

Although there were four states during the period of warring states that succeeded in expanding their territories through offensive warfare, Mozi reminds us that there were ten thousand other small states involved in wars which became extinct. This proves that offensive war is an unsuccessful strategy in ordering a state. War is likened to a drug that proves beneficial only to some and is, therefore, not effective (Watson 1963, 59). It is, however, interesting to note that an eloquent statesman like Mozi, who argued rigorously against warfare, still supported a just war against tyrant rulers. When the sage kings engaged in war, it was not offensive but "punishment" and they merely acted as Heaven's human instruments (Watson 1963, 56). This pragmatic position is universal in Chinese ancient writings.

As we can see, Mozi and both the Confucian *Analects* and the Daoist *Daodejing* support the idea of peace and nonviolence. Both traditions, based on pragmatic motives, are against warfare. War causes death and damage. Moreover, it is counterproductive and there is more lost than gained. Both traditions also reject war on the basis of their vision of government. For Confucians, it is a benevolent government that uses less force, and the Daoist favors the course of nature which uses no force. It is, therefore, clear that in the textual tradition of China there are ample supports for the pursuit of nonviolence and peacemaking.

To what extent and in what way these ideals are shared and carried out in Chinese villages of the South is our next concern. In our discussion of Chinese villages, we have chosen recent ethnographic reports from three representative locations. They are Heyuan of the Fujian province, Zhongyuan of the Jiangxi province, and Pingshi from the Guangdong province.

HEYUAN IN THE FUJIAN PROVINCE

Heyuan is the name of the river that runs through two counties in Fujian Province. Along the river, there are 13 villages comprised of some 10 major lineages. According to their lineage registers, the residents of the 13 villages came to the area between the period of the end of the Song (1279 C.E.) and the beginning of the Ming (1369 C.E.) dynasties. The 10 lineages can be loosely described as the Hakka people or the Guest People, meaning that they were immigrants from the North and spoke a related Hakka dialect. There is evidence to show that the original inhabitants of the area are *She* people, now a minority race in China. Challenge to the life of the Guest People comes from two fronts. One is from competition among the Guest people of different lineages for scarce resources. The other is from competition with the aboriginal people. As the field worker Yang Yanjie observes, compared with other areas, Heyuan has fewer conflicts and less violence between lineages and villages (Yang 1996, 271). A major factor accounting for peaceful relations between lineages in the Heyuan area is the rotating worship of their local god, Marquis Hehu.

There are at least two different versions with regard to the origin of the local god Marquis Hehu. According to the local gazette, Marquis Hehu was a local official who gave alms to the people during a famine. Upon his death, people built a temple in his memory. The oral tradition, however, presents Hehu as the spirit of a frog or a turtle who once helped the emperor of the Tang dynasty, Li Shimin (R.627-650 C.E.), to cross a river when his enemy pursued him. When Li became the emperor, Hehu was granted the title of Marquis. No matter what his origin, Hehu is very popular in the area. People call him grandpa (*gongtai*). Although there is a permanent temple for Marquis Hehu which is situated in the middle of the Heyuan area, the major ritual associated with the god consists of rotating worship. This means that the statue of the god is circulated among the 13 villages in Heyuan for worshipping.

The rotating worship of the god starts with the celebration of his birthday, on the second of February of the lunar calendar. The birthday of the god is an occasion for the people of the 13 villages to gather together in the temple of the god. A one-day, elaborate offering or *jiao* ritual is organized by the 13 villages. A *jiao* ritual is a Daoist ritual consisting of lavish sacrifices to local gods and spirits, adopted and performed by local Daoists (Lagerwey 1987, 20-21). A committee formed by representatives of the 13 villages oversees all the details of the event.

The order of circulation varies in the course of time but the principle remains the same. The statue of the god is taken, in turn, to stay in one village for one year. Therefore, after the joint celebration of the god's birthday, the village whose turn it is to receive the god will take the statue of the god back to their village. Before they take the god back home, the god will first be taken on a big parade to the market of the village, then on to neighbouring villages. Yang reports that the people joining the parade sometimes form a line as long as two to three kilometers (Yang 1996, 257). After the parade, the god will be brought back to the lineage hall of the hosting village. Depending on whether the village is multi-lineage, the god will take turns staying in different lineage halls in the village. During the stay of the god, the responsibility for worshipping is divided among the branches of each lineage. Within each branch, every family will be assigned one to two days, depending on the size of the family, and will be held responsible for the worshipping of the god. The responsibility includes hiring a team of musicians to play music in the lineage hall and offering pork and chicken, the best food in a Chinese village, to the god. Above all, the family has to be a host to a dinner of 10 to 20 tables, inviting guests from the village.

During his one year stay in the village, the god will be visited by other villages on two occasions. Because of its large area geographically, Heyuan is divided into upper and lower sections. When the god stays in one of the five villages situated in the upper parts, all five villages come to visit the god with lanterns on the fifteenth of the first lunar month, that is, the Yuanxiao festival. The same applies to the eight villages in the lower Heyuan. Visiting of the god coincides with the celebration of the Yuanxiao festival. On the fifteenth day of August, the village that will receive the god in the next year has to come to visit the god.

On the first day of February, one day before the birthday of the god, the one-year stay of the god in the village ends. The god will be sent back to the temple. Thirteen villages will come together again for the performing of another elaborate *jiao* ritual. An important joint meeting of the representatives from the 13 villages will be held to discuss any matters arising from the rotating worship. Then, on the second of February, comes the celebration of the god's birthday, which also marks the beginning of another cycle of rotating worship. The god will be taken to stay for another year in a village.

The key to peace in Heyuan is the human tie created through the worship of their local god, Marquis Hehu. As we have seen, the rotating worship of their local god requires complex organization. It involves all levels of cooperation and collaboration. The celebration of the god's birthday is a joint function of the 13 villages. An organizing committee has to be formed by representatives from the 13 villages. While the god is taking turns to stay in each of the 13 villages, neighboring villages have to organize visits to the god. During the stay of the god in each village, every family takes turns to organize a banquet for the god and for their fellow villagers. It is through the rotating worship that the 13 villages are brought together to strengthen the ties both within each village and among the 13 villages. We will see below that the role of local religion in maintaining the peace of the region is prominent in South China.

ZHONGFANG OF THE JIANGXI PROVINCE

In a valley 10 kilometers east of the Yudu county seat in the Gannan region of Jiangxi Province, there is a group of 15 villages known as *wuchang* (house area). During the time of the Republic of China (1912-1949), this region was called Zongfang. Each village is uni-lineage and there are altogether eight different lineages. The Zeng lineage occupies seven out of the 15 villages while the Li lineage occupies two. Six other lineages occupy one village each.

According to the fieldwork report by Ziyu (Ziyu 1997, 106), the two dominant lineages, Zeng and Li, have a history of conflicts. Ziyu describes a recent conflict between the two lineages. One Zeng family member built a flat yard for his drying of grains near the border of two villages inhabited by Zeng and Li. The Li protested on the basis of geomantic influence, and a fight was about to break out. This was resolved as a result of reconciliation efforts by a member of the Li family. It is worth noticing that conflicts do not lead to armed fights or bloodshed according to the report. An explanation again may be found in the local religion of the area.

The 15 villages worship three popular local gods known together as the three grandpas: Zhang, Gao, and Lai gong. Zhang and Lai gong were dressed as civil officials while Gao gong was a military official. Both Gao and Lai gong died martyrs in the cause of justice. When Gao was a military official, the prince oppressed his people. Gao fought against the prince with his army but was killed by the prince. Legend has it that Gao eventually became a god.

Lai gong was a civil official killed by a boatman who extorted money from him on his trip crossing a river. Lai was killed because he refused to yield to the wicked boatman. Comparatively speaking, there are many more stories circulated about the Zhang gong than Gao and Lai gong. He was a Daoist trained in Mt. Qi. He engaged in a contest of magic with another local Daoist, Hanyi gong. Zhang deeply moved the old mother of Mt. Qi, a divine instructress, by drinking up the water used to wash her wounded leg. She eventually taught Zhang to become an immortal. Despite his becoming an immortal, Zhang likes to turn himself into a big-headed fun-loving god who goes out to play with 12-year-old children, thereby preventing them from doing their adult-defined duties. Zhang is best described as an "unruly god" (Shahar and Weller 1996).

The three grandpas have a temple, and their worship centers on their temple festival which is in May and lasts for half a month. The 15 villages take turns receiving the gods in sedan chairs into their lineage hall where they stay for one night. The date on which the gods arrive is so important that the traditional Dragon Boat festival (Duanwu) is celebrated at the same time. This means that the festival of each village is different, and it changes each year as the order in which the village receives the gods is determined by rotation.

The most exciting part of the temple festival of the three grandpas is the ritual that takes place just before the gods are passed on to the neighbors. It is called *lian pusa* (refining the gods or practicing with the gods) and is also known as *zaying* (to set up the base camp)

(Ziyu 1997, 109). Five flags with different colors are set up in four directions. The sedan chairs on which the gods are seated are carried by youths zigzagging through the flags. The youths wear no clothes on the upper part of their bodies in order to show off their muscles. They only carry one handle of the sedan chair to allow maximum shaking of the chairs. Running ahead of them is another youth carrying a flag. Should he not run fast enough, the youths carrying the sedan chairs will crash into him with their chairs. The running is accompanied by loud shouting, which shows the strength and power of the gods and the people carrying them. It is important to recognize this ritual in the context of the many conflicts between the villages, especially between the two biggest lineages, Zeng and Li. The noise and muscular demonstration of the ritual can then be understood as the channelling and symbolizing of the conflicts and clashes between neighbouring lineages.

The conflict and tension arises from scarce resources among the 15 villages in Zongfang of Yudu. Although conflict seems to be inevitable, armed conflict and bloodshed are avoided. The eight lineages, although competing for scarce resources, manage to live peacefully together. Again, the key for peace is to be found in the rotating worship of a local god. Unlike Heyuan, the god in Zhongfang of Yudu is circulated and stays in each village only for one day. The half-month event of the god's temple festival is an occasion for the 15 villages to come together to coordinate the circulation of the god's statue. As we have pointed out, the ritual involved in passing the god's statue from one village to another expresses conflicts between villages symbolically, in a non-harmful way. The ritual, therefore, functions as a safety valve for the 15 villages.

THE PINGSHI OF GUANGDONG PROVINCE

The Pingshi township is situated on the border between two provinces, Hunan and Guangdong, and it acts as a trans-shipment center for the two provinces. While people in Hunan supply pigs for Guangzhou, the capital of Guangdong, they rely on Guangzhou for imports of salt. Before the building of a railway in 1933, goods were shipped back and forth between Guangzhou and Pingshi by using the Wu River. According to residents still living in Pingshi (Tam 1998), in the past, there were more than a hundred ships docked along the river in Pingshi every day. Because of the intense commercial activities, a commercial street one-and-a-half kilometers long with more than two hundred shops was developed along the Wu River in Pingshi. Most owners of the shops lived on the second floor of the shops, forming a community of about a thousand people. Surrounding the commercial street were 80 villages with 42 lineages. According to one old person living on the street, there used to be a lineage hall on the street that housed the tablets of ancestors of the 42 lineages. Apparently there was joint ancestor worship, details of which are forgotten. Of the 42, there were 10 dominating lineages. Representatives of the 10 lineages would meet in the street at an interval of between two to five years to resolve any conflicts arising between the lineages. Despite the complex mixture of lineages in the street, there were never any armed fights, conflicts, or bloodshed among lineages living in the area.

Just as there is a mixture of lineages from different provinces in Pingshi, there is also a complicated mixture of temples in the area. Unfortunately, not a single one survived the Cultural Revolution (1966-1976). There had been a temple for one of the most popular gods in Guangdong—Guandi. There is also a temple for the famous Mazu goddess in Fujian. There were altogether some 20 temples in the area. On the commercial street itself, there were six major temples. In addition, there were three chambers of commerce: one for Jiangxi, one for Hunan, and one for Guangdong provinces. All of the chambers of commerce had statues of their local gods and they functioned partly as a temple. Among the six temples in the street, the temple for the General god was the most popular. According to the legend, the General god was a general in the Eastern Han dynasty (24-220 C.E.) who was sent to the South to fight the Barbarian. He died in the war, and the people built a temple to commemorate him.

Pingshi has become a famous tourist spot for boat-drifting in China, owing to the strong current of the Wu River. While people today seek excitement by drifting down the stream, people in the past risked their lives in transporting goods on the river to and from Guangzhou and Pingshi. At the start of every trip, all boatmen would go to worship in the temple of the General who protected them from accidents on the river.

The climax of worship for the General god remained its temple festival. It was held in conjunction with eight other major temples in the area. Every temple had its own temple festivals but all of them would join in the celebration of other temple festivals. Therefore, the eight temples took turns in hosting a temple festival. Four of the eight temples were in the commercial street: the temple for the General (Jiangjun), the temple of the three worlds (Sanjie) with Guandi as the main deity, the temple for officials of the altar (Tangong), and the temple for the returning dragon (Huilong) with Mazu as the main deity. The other four temples were in the neighbouring villages: Liantang, Guitang, Tangkou, and Shuinui wan. The names of gods in these temples have mostly been forgotten as these temples failed to survive the Cultural Revolution in the sixties. The celebrations of the temple festivals were quite uniform. A parade would first be organized by representatives from major lineages in Pingshi, which visited all the eight temples. During the procession, the god who was celebrating a birthday led the line while the other seven gods followed behind. Then, there was an elaborate *jiao* ritual consisting of sacrifices and deliverance of the souls of those who had a violent death or who died without offspring.

The case of Pingshi once again has shown the role of local religion in lineage alliance, which contributes substantially to peace in the region. Pingshi's economy is different from other traditional Chinese villages in that commerce has replaced the traditional economy of agriculture. It is a community of multi-lineages with different places of origin. Yet, the mechanism for resolving potential conflicts among lineages remains the same as in other areas. Although they do not share a single local god, residents of Pingshi organize joint religious functions, thereby bringing together people of different faiths. Joint ancestor worship not only strengthens the ties among the 42 lineages but also creates an occasion to discuss problems and resolve conflicts between lineages. Joint temple festivals also help to bring people together and strengthen their ties.

CONCLUSION

We have studied three different locations in South China where there are, due to scarce resources, either existing or potential conflicts and tensions among lineages living in the area. Armed conflicts and bloodshed are, however, avoided because of the existence of an informal mechanism that prevents and channels conflicts. This mechanism is provided by the temple festivals of their local religion. A temple festival basically celebrates the birthday of a god. It is an elaborate event that calls for cooperation from different lineages in the region. An organizing committee that consists of representatives from different lineages has to be set up. Often this committee provides an occasion for discussion of interests, settling of differences, and resolution of disputes.

A large-scale parade is the climax for every temple festival. The parade allows each lineage to organize its own troop, be it for a lion dance, dragon dance, or other performance. The parade is often a demonstration of the strength of a lineage. The strength of a lineage is shown by the extravagance of its performance and the number of male youths participating in the parade. Field observation tells us that the noisy and powerful procession in the temple festival also functions as a safety valve for a non-harmful symbolic expression of conflicts and clashes among lineages.

Another salient element of the temple festival is its communal character. Not only will representatives of lineages come together for the occasion but also every single member of the community will come. All participate in the festival and enjoy the carnival spirit of the event that obviously helps to ease tension and subvert hatred arising from competition for scarce resources in daily life. The coming together of the whole community generates a community spirit which is heightened by the entertainment provided by the festival, including theatrical productions which are a must in every single temple festival.

The elite Confucian and Daoist traditions support the position of nonviolence, and the people at the grassroots level realize the ideal of nonviolence through their practice of local religion. Faith in their local gods has helped the Chinese people to work together with their competitors for scarce resources. Their faith challenges them to act fairly and to share equally the responsibility to serve the gods. In serving their gods, the Chinese people strive to enlarge their brotherhood and sisterhood beyond family lineage. Religion also provides a basis for creative cooperation and coexistence of lineages in a region.

Temple festivals become the key for regional peace in China as they help to express and channel inter-lineage conflicts and tensions in symbolic but non-harmful ways. Temple festivals also call for creative and democratic cooperation among neighboring lineages which is realized in the form of rotating worship. It is local temple festivals which help to maintain regional peace and prevent destructive bloodshed and armed conflicts among lineages. In this connection, temple festivals could be developed as "social capital" (Bourdieu 1983, 248) which produces profit in the form of regional stability and tourist attraction.

Lineage alliance and regional identity based on local religion can be a resource for reconciliation and peacemaking as well as a potential weapon for inter-communal conflict (Lamley 1990). Armed conflicts and bloodshed among lineages are not well documented in China. They are, therefore, difficult to study. In the history of Taiwan, armed conflict between Cantonese and Hakka people based on regional, cultural, and religious differences is a well known occurrence (Ino 1965, 929-957). Some have claimed that, since the Qing dynasty (1644-1912 C.E.), on average, there has been an armed battle every eight years (Committee of Historical Documents in Taiwan Province 1979, 420).

The dual function of lineage alliance as the root of nonviolence and yet as a fuel for conflict calls for further studies and research. This dual function can be a resource for reconciliation and peacemaking as well as a potential weapon for inter-communal conflict (Lamley 1990).

ANNOTATED BIBLIOGRAPHY

Bourdieu, Pierre. "The Forms of Capital." In *Handbook of Theory and Research for the Sociology of Education*, ed. John G. Richardson, trans. Richard Nice, 241-258. New York: Greenwood Press, 1986.

Chan, Wing-tsit. *A Sourcebook in Chinese Philosophy*. New Jersey: Princeton University Press, 1963.

Confucius. *The Analects*. Trans. D.C. Lau. New York: Penguin Books, 1970.

Creel, Herrlee G. *What is Taoism? And Other Studies in Chinese Cultural History*. Chicago: University of Chicago Press, 1970.

Ino, Kanori. *Taiwan Bunkashi* (Cultural Monograph of Taiwan). Tokyo: Tokoshoin, 1965. Ino's book contains one chapter that deals with regional armed conflict in Taiwan. It enables us to see the dual function of lineage and regional alliance in Chinese society, namely as both resource for reconciliation and violent conflict.

Lagerwey, John. Preface to *Meizhou diqu de miaohui yu zongzu* (Temple Festivals and Lineage in Meizhou), ed. Fang Xuejia. Hong Kong: International Hakka Studies Association, Overseas Chinese Archives, and Ecole Francaise d'Extreme-Orient, 1996. This series, which will have 10 volumes, contains one of the most updated ethnographic reports on traditional rural society in South China. The series is a product of Lagerwey's project on the structure and dynamics of Chinese rural society. The project studies Chinese society through traditional religious festivals and it provides ample primary source for research in peace and nonviolence in Chinese society. Although all essays are written in Chinese, Lagerwey has provided the readers with a helpful summary in English in the beginning of each volume. Essays written in English to review volume one to five of the series are planned for publication in a conference volume, *Ethnography in China Today: A Critical Assessment of Methods and Results,* ed. Professor Daniel Overmyer.

————. *Taoist Ritual in Chinese Society and History.* New York: MacMillan Publishing, 1987.

Lamley, Harry J. "Lineage Feuding in Southern Fujian and Eastern Guangdong Under Qing Rule." In *Violence in China: Essays in Culture*, ed. Jonathan N. Lipman and Stevan Harrell. Albany: State University of New York Press, 1990.

Lopez, Donald S. Jr., ed. *Religions of China in Practice.* Princeton: Princeton University Press, 1996.

Lowe, Scott. *Mo Tzu's Religious Blueprint for a Chinese Utopia: The Will and the Way.* Lewiston/Queenston/Lampeter: The Edwin Mellen Press, 1992. Lowe's book is a helpful study on Mozi, who put forward the first systematic argument against offensive warfare in Chinese history. Lowe's book contains a summary of Mozi's argument and critical discussion on other studies on Mozi.

Mencius. Trans. D.C. Lau. New York: Penguin Books, 1970.

Redfield, Robert. *Peasant Society and Culture: An Anthropological Approach to Civilization.* Chicago & London: University of Chicago Press, 1956.

Shahar, Meir and Robert P. Weller, ed. *Unruly Gods: Divinity and Society in China.* Honolulu: University of Hawai'i Press, 1996.

Taiwan sheng wenxian weiyuan hui (Committee of Historical Documents in Taiwan Province). *Taiwan shi* (History of Taiwan). Taipei: Zhongwen tushu guan, 1979.

Tam, Wai Lun. "Yuebei diqu Lao pingshi zhen laojie di shequ jiegou yu zongjiao wenhua" (The Social Structure, Commerce and Religious Culture of the Old Street in the Lao Pingshi Township in Northern Guangdong). Paper presented at the Second International Conference on Hakkaology, Institute of Ethnology, Academia sinica, Taipei, November 6, 1998. This paper as well as the section on Pingshi of the present chapter is based on the author's fieldwork studies conducted in Pingshi during the months of July and December 1997.

Teiser, Stephen F. "The Spirits of Chinese Religion." In *Religion of China in Practice,* ed. Donald Lopez, 3-37. Princeton: Princeton University Press, 1996.

Tzu, Lao. *Tao Te Ching.* Trans. D.C. Lau. New York: Penguin Books, 1963.

Tzu, Mo. *Basic Writings.* Trans. Burton Watson. New York: Columbia University Press, 1963.

Yang, Yanjie. *Minxi kejia zonzu shehui yanjiu* (Field Studies of Hakka Lineage Society in Minxi). Hong Kong: International Hakka Studies Association, Overseas Chinese Archives, and Ecole Francaise d'Extreme-Orient, 1996. Yang's book is the only book in the series written by one author. It contains precious information and analysis of Hakka lineage and society in Minxi. Yang's study on the rotating worship—a sociological pattern in the Hakka countryside—represents a pioneering study on the subject.

Ziyu (Li Yaohua). *Zhongfang sangong yingshen jishi* (Welcoming the Sangong of Zhongfeng). In *Gannan diqu di miaohui yu zongzu* (Temple Festivals and Lineages in Gannan), ed. Luo Yong and John Lagerwey, 94-110. Hong Kong: International Hakka Studies Association, Overseas Chinese Archives, and Ecole Francaise d'Extreme-Orient, 1997. This volume of the series collects ethnographic essays in Gannan of Jiangxi Province. It contains wonderful reports of important temple festivals in different counties and villages. It is another important primary source for the study of how religious practice of temple festivals in China increases communication and cooperation, and thus reduces violence and conflicts. A review essay on this volume written by the present author will appear in the forthcoming conference volume, *Ethnography in China Today: A Critical Assessment of Methods and Results,* ed. Daniel Overmyer.

Chapter 4

AHIMSA AND THE UNITY OF ALL THINGS: A HINDU VIEW OF NONVIOLENCE

By Sunanda Y. Shastri and Yajneshwar S. Shastri

In order to speak of issues of war and peace in Hindu thought, it is imperative that one survey the classic literature on the subject of "*ahimsa*," which has developed over thousands of years on the Indian subcontinent. In Hindu traditions, nonviolence is termed *ahimsa*. *Ahimsa*, however, is not equivalent to pacifism, conscientious objection to war, or civil disobedience as understood in Western circles. It is a philosophical, religious, and ethical concept with a number of important connotations. *Ahimsa* is not used in a purely negative sense but is used as a positive antidote to violence.

Ahimsa is the negation of violence (*himsa*). One can see the wide range of *ahimsa* by noting the meanings of *himsa*:

- Treating one's self as different from others
- Failing to realize the fundamental unity of all beings
- Torturing or destroying one's own body by ignorance
- Causing pain to others
- Troubling others physically, mentally, or vocally
- Hurting or injuring others by speech, mind, and body
- Killing or separating the life force from the body of others

DR. YAJNESHWAR S. SHASTRI is chair of the Department of Philosophy and associate professor at the School of Psychology, Education, and Philosophy at Gujarat University, Ahmedabad, India. He has published numerous articles and books in Hindi and English on various aspects of Indian religion, including Buddhism, Jainism, and Hinduism, and is the author (in English) of *Traverses on Less Trodden Path of Indian Philosophy and Religion* (1991); *Foundations of Hinduism* (1993); *A Collection of Prayers* (1994); and *The Salient Features of Hinduism* (1994). He has been Scholar-in-Residence at Loyola Marymount University in 1993, 1994, and 1998.

DR. SUNANDA SHASTRI is assistant professor in Sanskrit in the Department of Sanskrit of Gujarat University, Ahmedabad. Her specialization is Sanskrit grammar and law studies. She wrote her Ph.D. dissertation on Dharma Shastra (Ancient Indian Law) and has published several papers in English, Hindi, and Marathi in national and international journals. She is the author of *Sanskrit for Beginners* (1994), now in its second edition, and taught Sanskrit at Loyola Marymount University in the summer of 1994.

- Destroying, knowingly or unknowingly, the properties and wealth of others
- Exhibiting hatred towards others
- Intimidating, beating, tying up, destroying and taking the livelihood of others
- Stealing the property or belongings of others
- Injuring other harmless beings for the sake of one's own pleasure
- Hurting innocent beings by using harsh words
- Oppressing or harassing people by levying undue taxes
- Cutting down the various (especially medicinal) trees and plants
- Acting against the wishes of parents and teachers
- Abusing students (by a teacher)
- Exploiting and taking unfair advantage of others, wrong thinking, and wrong action (*Rgveda* I.114.7; II.12.10, II.33.15; VII.104.7, 12, 16, 19; *Ishavasya Upanishad* 3; *Manusmruti*, I.29; IV.162; V.45; VII.285, 288, 293, 297, 310; XI.63; *Mahabharata Shantiparva*, 71.15; *Anushasanaparva*, XIII.113.8; 115.19; *Shabdakaipadruma, A Sanskrit Dictionary on* Ahimsa, n.d.)

The essence of all these various meanings of violence is that violence causes pain or suffering in one way or another. *Ahimsa* is an antidote to all these kinds of violence. But there is far more to *ahimsa* than merely non-hurting or non-killing. It includes giving up concepts of "otherness," "separateness," "selfishness," and "self-centeredness" and identifying oneself with all other beings.

Ahimsa is a positive doctrine of love, friendship, and equality among all living beings of the universe. This has as its basis the acceptance of the ultimate goodness of mankind. It renounces hatred and cultivates compassion based on a sense of oneness of all and feelings of kinship with all life forms. Therefore, according to Hindu tradition, *ahimsa* is to be understood as a mental attitude we cultivate toward others.

Sometimes, however, we may have to appear to be cruel and injurious even though our heart is full of love and kindness. Shakespeare beautifully expresses this in *Hamlet* when he says, "I am cruel only to be kind." Mothers sometimes may scold or beat their children, but their intention is not to hurt their children. It is to improve the children's behavior and make them good citizens. A surgeon may appear cruel and bloody while performing operations but his action cannot be called *himsa*. So, the concept of *ahimsa*, in

Hindu traditions, includes two ethical ideals: one is the pursuit of the good of humanity (*lokahita*) and the other is devotion to the good of all living beings and the environment (*sarvabhutahita*).

SPECIFIC TEXTS AND TRADITIONS WHICH SUPPORT THE POSITION OF NONVIOLENCE

The Four Vedas are the foundational scriptures of the Hindu culture. The earliest Veda is the *Rgveda* (*circa* 3000 B.C.) and it is believed to be the earliest poetic and religious document of the human race. The *Rgveda* uses the term *himsa* in the sense of physical injury and killing, and *ahimsa* in the sense of physical non-injury. Forgiveness is asked for committing violence towards others. It is also mentioned in the *Rgveda* that non-injury is beneficial in establishing friendship and cultivating a sense of oneness. The *Rgveda* also states that "man must protect other men from all sides." The spirit of nonviolence is seen in the immortal passages of *Rgveda* such as:

> Come together, talk together,
> Let our minds be in harmony.
> Common be our prayer,
> Common be our end,
> Common be our purpose,
> Common be our deliberations,
> Common be our desires,
> United be our hearts,
> United be our intentions,
> Perfect be the union among us. (*Rgveda* X.191.2-4)

In these passages, the unity of mankind is emphasized in order to maintain peace and harmony in the universe and society.

The *Yajurveda* declares that:

> May all beings look at me
> With friendly eye.
> May I look at all
> With friendly eye.
> May all look at one another
> With friendly eye. (*Yajurveda* XXXVI.18)

Yajurveda prohibits killing of animals and birds by stating: "No person should kill animals and birds helpful to all; rather by serving them one should attain happiness" (*Yajurveda* XIII.47).

In *Samaveda,* it is said that: "We slay no victims, we worship entirely by the repetition of the sacred verses" (*Samaveda* I.II. IX.2).

The *Atharvaveda* says:

Lord by your grace I keep
goodwill towards all,
known and unknown
human beings. (*Atharvaveda* XVII.1-7)

These Vedic statements clearly imply that to maintain peace, harmony, and friendship, we should give up hatred, violence, and a sense of separateness.

The Vedic philosophy provides a theoretical basis for performing nonviolence by reflecting a vibrant, encompassing worldview which looks upon all objects in the universe, living and so-called non-living, as being rooted in and pervaded by one divine power, *Sat.* (*Sat.* literally means absolute or ultimate reality). In this universe everything is interconnected, interrelated, and interdependent. All things are a manifestation of that one supreme power or spirit, the great forces—the earth, the sky, the wind, fire, oceans, as well as various orders of life including human beings, plants, trees, animals. All are bound to each other within the great rhythms of nature. There is an organic unity in the whole universe. This idea is beautifully described in one of the hymns of the *Rgveda* (X.90.1-4).

According to *Upanishadic* literature (*Vedanta*), everything in the universe is rooted in pure-consciousness and pervaded by pure-consciousness. The *Vedanta* declares the spiritual unity of all existence in categorical terms by stating that, "In this cosmos, whatever exists—living and non-living—all that is, is pervaded by one divine consciousness" (*Ishavasya Upanishad* 1). This all-pervasive nature of Brahman or ultimate reality is beautifully described in several *Upanishads.* The *Mundaka-Upanishad,* for example, states:

Indeed, this Brahman (pure-consciousness)
is the Immortal Being.
In front is Brahman, behind is Brahman.
It is to the right and to the left.
It spreads forth above and below,
Indeed, Brahman is the effulgent universe. (*Mundaka Upanishad* II.II.12)

The *Aitereya Upanishad* declares, "The Reality behind all these things of the universe is the Brahman, which is pure-consciousness. All things are established in consciousness, work through consciousness, and their foundation is consciousness" (III.V.3). "All that is, is Brahman," says *Chandogya Upanishad* (III.XIV.1). The *Taittiriya Upanishad* clearly states that: "There is an all-pervading higher reality—Brahman, out of which we are born and to which we will ultimately return (III.1.6). The *Svetasvatara Upanishad* also establishes the close relationship between the divinity—Brahman—and the external universe, identifying natural phenomena with the Brahman, from which all the worlds sprang (IV.II.3-4).

One could continue with dozens, if not hundreds, more texts along these lines, but the general point is clear, namely, that the sense of duality or separateness is the root cause of hatred and violence. Therefore, the *Ishavasya Upanisad* advises us to see one's own self in everything and everything in one's own self. Then we will not hate anyone (6). In loving others we are loving ourselves, and when hurting others we are hurting ourselves, because we all carry the same divinity. Once this unity of all is realized, it is thought that there will be no sorrow, no grief, and no delusion, and peace will prevail in the heart of every being (7). The essence of the Vedantic notion then is that the Brahman, the pure-consciousness, is inseparable from its manifestations. To hurt or violate any creature or object in nature is to hurt or violate Brahman itself. This notion of fundamental sameness is the basis for nonviolent action towards all. Killer and killed: both are divine from the perspective of this classic.

The term *ahimsa* is also used in a moral sense in several texts of the Hindu tradition. The first reference to *ahimsa* in a moral sense is found in *Kapisthalakathasamhita*, which is a pre-*Upanishadic* reference. Here, there is a reference to the non-killing of animals in sacrifice (XXXI.11). The *Chandogya Upanishad* uses the word *ahimsa* in the list of religious virtues, such as truthfulness, nonviolence, austerity, straightforwardness, and charity (III.17.4). *Ahimsa* should be practiced by one who desires to attain the world of Brahman and not to "return again" (VII.14.1). In later *Upanishads* the practice of *ahimsa* is glorified. "Seeing an all-pervading self in everything is the highest form of *ahimsa*," says *Jabaladarshana Upanishad* (I.8). "It is the practice of *ahimsa* which takes one to the state of immortality," states *Naradaparivrajakopanishad* (III.45). The *Shandilya Upanishad* defines *ahimsa* as "not to cause pain to any living beings at any time either mental, vocal, or physical" and says that it is one of the ten moral restraints, strictly to be followed by yogis (I.1).

Nonviolence is glorified in the later texts of classical literature of the Hindu tradition. These texts might have been influenced by the ascetic and yogic traditions. In the *Ramayana* of Valmiki, one of the great epics of the Hindus, it is mentioned that the descendants of Rama (the race of the Ikshvaku) are the lovers of *ahimsa* (V.31.4). The *Mahabharata*, another great Hindu epic composed by Vyasa, contains an extensive discussion of the importance of *ahimsa* and also provides a concise philosophical definition of *ahimsa* from the Hindu perspective. It says, "Action which is against one's own desires should also not be done to others. One should never do that to another which one regards as injurious to one's own self. Therefore, one should treat all others as one's own self" (XIII.113-8.115-19). One who does not injure or does not take away the lives of living beings is not bound by karma (*Shantiparva* 277). It is important to note that the "golden rule," namely, that "One should never do that to another which one considered undesirable for oneself," was formulated in *Mahabharata* long before the rabbinic and Christian era.

According to the *Mahabharata*, the practice of *ahimsa* is a duty which is complete with respect to its reward (*Shantiparva* 272, 20). The merit of a man practicing *ahimsa* is said to be inexhaustible and enables one to become free from all sins (XIII.116.41; *Shantiparva* 35.37). An action which is done with violence kills faith and, faith being destroyed, it ruins the man. The merit of other penances is destroyed if one practices *himsa* (*Shantiparva* 192.17, 246.6). Thus, *ahimsa* is the highest form of religion, virtue, and duty (*ahimsa paramodharmah*).

The *Anushasanaparva* of the *Mahabharata* beautifully describes the merit and importance of *ahimsa* in several verses. In these passages, *ahimsa* is exalted as the best of all actions, giving birth to righteousness and serving as the best possible means of purification. The following few selected passages indicate the significance of nonviolence within a Hindu context:

> Those right-souled persons who desire beauty, faultlessness of limbs, long life, understanding, mental and physical strength, and memory should abstain from acts of violence. (XIII.115.8)

> *Ahimsa* is the path of righteousness. It is the highest purification. It is also the highest truth from which all *dharma*s (virtues) proceed. (XIII.125.25)

> *Ahimsa* is the highest *dharma* (virtue, duty). *Ahimsa* is the best austerity. *Ahimsa* is the greatest gift. *Ahimsa* is the highest self-control. *Ahimsa* is the highest sacrifice. *Ahimsa* is the highest power. *Ahimsa* is the highest friend. *Ahimsa* is the highest truth. *Ahimsa* is the highest teaching. (XIII.116.37-41)

Here again, as we have noted in other texts, it is stated that *ahimsa* really means seeing or treating others as one's own self, giving up a sense of separateness:

> That person who indeed sees being as
> like his own self, who has cast aside the stick,
> and whose anger is conquered, prospers happily
> in the life to come. (XIII.114.6)

> Even the gods are bewildered at the path
> of the one who seeks the abode of no abode,
> who sees all beings with the being of oneself
> as that of all beings. (XIII.114.7)

> From not holding to the other
> as opposite from oneself
> there is the essence of *dharma*. (XIII.114.8)

The *Bhagavadgita*, the famous philosophical text of the Hindus (which is part of the *Mahabharata*), does in certain circumstances support war and violence to remove injustice and evil forces from society, and to purify society. Philosophically, however, the text repeats the themes previously noted by asking spiritual aspirants to look on all as analogous with one's own self (VI.32) and that one should commit no violence, thinking that the lord or divinity is in everything (XI.34, IV.27).

Bhagavadgita mentions *ahimsa* as one of the divine qualities, which is to be cultivated and practiced by one and all (XVI.2,

XVII.14). Sri Shankaracharya, the greatest exponent of Advaita philosophy (non-dualism), when commenting on the *Bhagavadgita*, said that a yogi should be nonviolent towards others and should identify the self of all beings with his own. Also, he should do only to others that which is desirable and pleasant to his own self, but should refrain from doing that to others which is undesirable and unpleasant for himself (VI.32).

Yogasutra of Patanjali mentions *ahimsa* as the basis of ethical practices, a universal principle which is to be practiced by one and all irrespective of religion, race, creed, and sex. It is said that if *ahimsa* is practiced and mastered, total enmity disappears from one's mind and heart, and others also give up hatred in the proximity of one practicing *ahimsa*. (II.35). One must practice *ahimsa* in its broadest sense—unrestricted by caste, place, time, and circumstances. *Ahimsa* here is required as the foremost virtue by aspiring yogis. Yogic *ahimsa* here means absence of oppression towards all beings, in all respects, and for all times (Vyasa on *Yogasutra* II.30-32).

Ancient Hindu law and sociological texts also uphold the practice of *ahimsa*. The Laws of *Manu* (*Manusmruti*), which influenced and shaped Hindu society for a long period, include *ahimsa* as one of the characteristics of *dharma*—a duty, the path of righteousness and cardinal virtue, which is to be followed by all (X.63). It must be practiced for the welfare of all human beings (II.158). *Manu* further states that violence disturbs one's mind and results in ill-health whereas nonviolence brings sound health (XI.52). The Laws of *Manu* prohibit meat-eating for higher classes (Brahmins—intellectuals, thinkers, and priests) and encourage other classes of people not to eat meat. The laws of *Manu* state that the merit of not eating meat by killing or causing the killing of animals is equal to the merit of hundreds of horse sacrifices (V.53). According to *Manu*, "Immortality is the highest fruit of *ahimsa*" (VI.60). Several other ancient Hindu law texts, such as *Bodhayanadharmasutra*, *Yajnavalkyasmruti*, and others, glorify the merit of practicing *ahimsa*. According to these texts, *ahimsa* is a kind of internal purification (*Bodhayana* III.1-23) and by its practice one accumulates good karmic consequences (*Yajnavalkyasmruti* I.8, I.122).

It is interesting to note that though these ancient legal texts glorify the practice of nonviolence, they consider that killing animals in sacrifice does not qualify as violence. The laws of *Manu* add that the killing of animals prescribed in the sacrifice should be construed to mean *ahimsa* because the laws have Vedic sanction, and moral duties spring from the Vedas. Vedic *himsa* is morally equal to *ahimsa* in the sense that both produce the same good result. Animal sacrifice brings good for all (V.41,44; VI.12). Commentators and other lawmakers justified *Manu* and allowed the eating of meat obtained through ritual sacrifice.

NONVIOLENCE AND VEGETARIANISM IN HINDU THOUGHT

The case of animal sacrifice actually serves to illustrate Hindu debates and principles related to the conception of violence and nonviolence. It is a common misconception that the entire ancient Hindu tradition supported animal sacrifice and meat-eating as part the sacrificial process. The Vedic or Hindu tradition as a whole never supported animal killings in sacrifice. Animal sacrifice was vehemently opposed by *Upanishadic* sages, philosophers, social thinkers, intellectuals, and literary persons from ancient times. A few ritualists, however, the followers of the path of ritualism known as *mimamsakas* or *karmakandins*, supported and practiced this animal sacrifice in the name of attaining heaven. When this ritualistic class became very powerful, they influenced the ancient Hindu lawmakers to accept killing animals in sacrifice and, ironically, to declare it as equal to nonviolence.

These bloody animal sacrifices did not fail to arouse criticism and protest. Even ancient Samaveda opposed this cruel act (I.II.IX.2). *Upanishadic* sages criticized not only animal-killing in sacrifice but questioned the merit or efficacy of performing sacrifice itself. In more than one place the *Upanishad* decries the value of sacrifice. *Upanishadic* seers treated all beings as essentially equal and considered the ritual as ineffective and meaningless. They felt it was far better to see the self (*atman*) in all beings than to perform even a hundred sacrifices. Performing any animal sacrifice is based on ignorance of the nature of self, and the "right knowledge" can dispel this ignorance. Right knowledge was considered the root of *ahimsa*.

Followers of the Sankhya system of philosophy opposed the *mimamsakas'* animal sacrifice in the name of religion; they called it

75

a sinful act, an impure act, which was based on *himsa*. They insisted it was irrational and baseless to say that animal sacrifice is not violence (*Sankhya Karika* I.2, 6.84; commentaries by Vachaspti Mishra and Vijnanabhikshu).

Even some commentators of *dharmashastras* (law texts) criticized animal sacrifice (Govindananda on Brahatmanu). In *Mahabharata* we find opposition to animal sacrifice: "Man loses merit earned from other penances by resorting to sacrificial killing. Men who are engaged in killing animals deserve to go to hell" (*Anushasanaparva*, XIII.69; *Shantiparva* 272.18). Opposition to animal sacrifice is found also in *purana* (mythology) literature, such as *Bhagavata* (I.9.52. V.26.25) and *Matsyapurana* (142.13). In the vast Hindu mythological literature (*puranas* consisting of 400,000 verses), the practice of *ahimsa* is praised. Ancient and very popular pauranic texts, such as *Agni, Bhagavata, Vishnu, Matsya, Kurma, Vayu,* and *Varaha*, are also full of the praise of *ahimsa*.

Although in the early period of Vedic civilization meat-eating was not strictly prohibited and vegetarianism was not strictly followed, by the time of the *Upanishadic* (classical), the killing of animals and birds for one's own pleasure and food was considered a great sin, and the practice of vegetarianism became the hallmark of the upper class. People like Brahmins and monks were prohibited from eating non-vegetarian food and liquor (*Manu* II.177). This strict vegetarianism is practiced today by the Brahmins of Hindu society. People of other classes were not prohibited from eating meat, but they were encouraged and advised not to eat meat by the glorification of the merit of non-killing of animals and birds and of not eating meat (Manu V.53). The *Mahabharata* criticizes meat-eating in the strongest terms: "The meat of other animals is like the flesh of one's own son. That foolish person, stupefied by folly, who eats meat is regarded as the vilest of human beings" (XIII.114.11). Such statements from the scriptures made a deep impact on the minds of the common people. Greater status was accorded to those who were able to follow a strict vegetarian diet. Even today, those who are allowed to eat non-vegetarian food in Hindu society do not eat meat daily. Occasionally they eat meat, but on certain days of the Hindu calendar they do not eat meat.

VEGETARIANISM AND ECOLOGICAL BALANCE

The practice of nonviolence in the form of vegetarianism is closely connected with the preservation of ecological balance. The *Yajurveda* lays down the rule that "no person should kill animals and birds helpful to all; rather, by serving them one should attain happiness" (XIII.47).

To preserve animal life, Hindu culture and religion associated different animals and birds with various gods and goddesses so that human beings would not kill them. It was also ordained in the Hindu tradition that one should not take food without also offering food to birds and animals, which is technically known as *Vaishvadevayajna*. *Vaishvadevayajna* is one of the daily observances that must be observed by all householders. This is still practiced by many adherents of Hindu tradition. Similarly, several plants, trees, and herbs are considered worthy of worship, and flowering and fruit-bearing trees are looked upon with great reverence and love and often considered equal to hundreds of children. Plants and flowers are associated with various gods and goddesses, so human beings may not cut and destroy them for the sake of quick money. Ancient Hindu law texts have prescribed several expiations and punishment for cutting trees.

In short, *ahimsa* in Hindu thought is so wide-ranging in its application that one can legitimately argue that the Earth is considered a Mother and a living presence. Hindus pray to Mother Earth in order to ask forgiveness for touching her with their feet, a prayer offered daily in the morning by every devout Hindu.

KARMA AND REBIRTH

The practice of nonviolence in Hindu tradition is also in some way linked to the doctrine of Karma and rebirth. According to this doctrine, every being reaps the fruits of his or her own deeds, whether good or bad, right or wrong. We reap what we sow. Bad deeds result in unpleasant consequences and good deeds in pleasant consequences. The result of all actions may not appear in this life so, to reap the fruits of past deeds, one has to take birth again. Each individual has to reap the fruits of his own actions. An individual's good and bad deeds decide his or her rebirth in a lower or higher category of life form. So, acts of nonviolence are considered as morally good deeds which bring happiness and cause birth in a higher category of life form. Acts of violence are morally bad and cause birth in a lower-category of life form.

The practice of nonviolence extends even to small life-forms— an idea that is deeply rooted in Hindu practice even today. For example, Hindu men and women generally do not use ant-killers; instead, they sprinkle turmeric powder to disperse ants or they gather them up to put them outside.

EXCEPTIONS TO THE PRACTICE OF NONVIOLENCE

The Hindu tradition accepts four stages of life: the stage of studenthood, the stage of householder, the retirement stage, and the stage of renunciation (monkhood). Applications of *ahimsa* to these stages also differ. *Ahimsa* is sometimes described as a common duty, sometimes as a specific duty. In the stage of studenthood, retirement, and monkhood, *ahimsa* must be practiced vigorously. In monkhood, it should be practiced absolutely, whereas, in the stage of a householder's life, a householder is exempted from following the absolute form of *ahimsa* because he has to compromise in order to fulfill his own specific duties. A householder cannot totally neglect his family, social responsibilities, and material well-being. It is impossible for a householder to practice *ahimsa* in any extreme degree so it has to be practiced in moderation in accordance with common sense and one's own family and social responsibility. The principal object is to maintain social order and the well-being of the people.

RELATIONS WITH THE WORLD

Hinduism is neither a dogma, nor a cult, nor a mere religion in a narrow sense. It is a culture, a way of life. It deals with all aspects of human existence. It does not repudiate the world and negate social values. Human life is considered a long journey towards perfection and, in this journey, natural desires and inclinations of man to possess and enjoy the good things of life cannot be overlooked. But everything must be in accordance with a moral and social order. Certain exceptions are mentioned with respect to practicing nonviolence. When an enemy attacks and kills hundreds of innocent beings or molests women, if one does nothing but stand back as a witness, this is not *ahimsa*; it is cowardice and weakness. One's duty is to fight and kill an enemy in such circumstances. If a beast enters into a cattleshed, one's duty is to kill the beast; otherwise, valuable cows will be killed. Fishermen may inflict injury on fish. This is required for their livelihood. A butcher's livelihood is based on killing some animals. So, their actions cannot be considered total violence. A warrior may kill his enemies on the battlefield because it is his duty to defend the country and to protect the people. The practice of *ahimsa* is not applicable in dealing with wicked people. So, the Hindu conception of *ahimsa* is universal, but its application is practical. Hindu nonviolence historically includes morally justifiable violence.

THE RELATION OF PEACE AND NONVIOLENCE WITHIN THE HINDU TRADITION

In the Hindu tradition, the term *shanti* is used for peace. The word *peace* is understood in two senses: One is spiritual peace and the other is peace in society and nature. The attainment of spiritual peace is considered the highest goal of human existence. This spiritual peace can be achieved through giving up a sense of separateness and plurality and identifying one's own self with all other beings in the universe (*Ishavasya Upanishad* 6-7). Eternal peace belongs to those who see unity or oneness behind all modifications of the universe (*Kathopanishad* V.13). The concept of duality is considered the root cause of violent action. The Hindu tradition hopes and aspires toward peace for all beings. The Vedas declare, "May there be peace in plants, trees, earth, directions, fire, water, wind, air, sky, heaven, animals, and human beings" (*Yajurveda*). The idea of peace in Hindu tradition is clearly evident from the daily prayers of devout Hindus which state, "May everyone be happy, may everyone be free from diseases, may everyone see good fortune, and may no one be unhappy" (Y.S. Shastri 1994, 72).

It is important to note that to establish peace in society, ancient Hindu lawmakers pointed out in several places (*Manusmruti, Naradasmruti*) that social peace can be established with the help of strict laws and punishments. If everyone were virtuous, good, honest, and nonviolent, there would be no need for any laws as such; however, since this is not so, society needs laws and punishments to bring peace into society.

THE ROLE OF WAR, PEACE, AND NONVIOLENCE IN HINDU TRADITION

The Hindu tradition has always held a balanced view about nonviolence and war. It always adopted rational and practical ways to maintain the social order, peace, and the well-being of all the people. Its final aim was to achieve spiritual peace, but it never neglected material well-being and social harmony. Whenever there was a rise of evil forces in society, Hindus first tried to establish peace through applying peaceful means, but when this attempt failed, they took the path of war to purify society. War against evil forces and violence against anti-social elements such as criminals is not considered nonviolence but a duty. Soldiers on the battlefield who kill their enemies do not engage in *himsa*, but are carrying out a professional duty—a duty toward one's own country, culture, and society—and this duty is considered an act of heroism. One must not allow evil forces to conquer society. Man must not be a mute witness to evils and injustice.

In Vedic literature, war against wicked persons, evil forces, and untruth is praised as an act of purification (*Rgveda* VIII.104.1, 7, 12, 13, 19). The victory of truthfulness is glorified. The *Bhagavadgita* considers war as one of the solutions to purify society. In present day Hindu society, there is a feeling, especially among the younger generation, that Indians have had enough talk of nonviolence. We have preached nonviolence in India for thousands of years. But in the modern world, perhaps we must rise to the call of Lord Krishna in the *Bhagavadgita* to be strong, powerful, and prepared for war, if the occasion demands. In this age of competition and wickedness, nonviolence seems to carry no weight. This is why 90 percent of the Indian population supported the recently conducted nuclear tests.

In spite of glorifying the practice of nonviolence by Hindu texts and tradition for thousands of years, there is still violence towards the weaker elements of society—women, the lower classes, and animals. This was true in ancient times but has continued in intensified forms to the present day. Women have continued to suffer great violence. In a world where there is a great desire for luxuries and where there is rampant consumerism, there are increased pressures on women to provide ever greater dowries. This practice has led to excessive violence against women. In addition, poor people are harassed, deprived of rights, and often treated as "untouchables"—a great blot on the otherwise glorious civilization of the Hindus.

In the name of industrialization and modernization, forests and hundreds of wild animals have been destroyed and water has been polluted with industrial wastes and chemicals, killing many living beings. The pressures of consumerism and self-centeredness have led to riots and increased hatred across community lines.

A YEARNING FOR PEACE

Every tradition in the world talks about peace. This talk of love for peace has been going on for thousands of years but, in spite of it, human history tells us that in every tradition there have been wars. War is not advisable, but preparation for war is going on everywhere. The whole world wants peace, yet the whole world prepares for war.

The *Ramayana* and the *Mahabharata*, the two great epics of the Hindus, depict the story of war and its terrible consequences and the importance of peace. In *Ramayana*, war was conducted as a struggle between good and evil, truth and untruth. Rama, the hero of the epic, represents righteousness, truthfulness, honesty, dutifulness, compassion, self-control, faithfulness, humility, courage, generosity, and non-anger. Ravana, the villain of the great epic, though highly learned, represents passion, vanity, egocentricism, arrogance, vainglory, anger, and ambition. His life is governed by passion and sex. The consequence of that war was the destruction of many lives and, ultimately, the destruction of the race of Ravana. Peace was established not through peaceful means but by violence and war.

In the *Mahabharata*, a horrendous 18-day war is described. In this large-scale war, kings of the entire Indian subcontinent were involved. Hundreds of thousands of heroes, kings, soldiers, great masters in archery and weapons, elephants, and horses were killed in 18 days. The war was fought between two cousins but it was also a war between good and evil forces. Lord Krishna tried to prevent the war through a peace treaty. He tried to tell Kauravas about the tragic consequences of war. But his efforts were in vain. War was inevitable. Even Arjuna, the war hero of the *Mahabharata* (one of the Pandavas), was horrified by the thought of war. On the battlefield, he was reluctant to fight. He implored Lord Krishna to stop the war. At that juncture, Lord Krishna advised him to perform his duty as a warrior, either to win the fight against evil forces in society or to die in the attempt. He convinced Arjuna that there cannot be ultimate peace without war. The result of this war was that it devoured a large portion of the population, left untold miseries for widows and children, and created millions of orphans.

The wars of the two great epics point out that peace cannot necessarily be established by peaceful means and thus suggest to many Hindus that sometimes war is necessary.

HINDU HEROES WHO EXEMPLIFY THE NONVIOLENT TRADITION

Despite this allowance for "justified war," thousands of wise men and women saints, sages, religious leaders, and poets have preached and followed the path of nonviolence. Hindu scriptures are full of their stories. The lives of Sri Chaitanya Mahaprabhu and Mahatma Gandhi are the best examples of the practice of nonviolence in the recent Hindu past.

Chaitanya Mahaprabhu (fifteenth to sixteenth centuries) lived according to the principle of *ahimsa*. His way of propagating nonviolence was chanting the glory of Lord. In his lifetime, he converted many cruel people who later became compassionate beings. The story is told that once Chaitanya Mahaprabhu heard that hundreds of cows and bulls were killed every year to feed the Muslim ruler of his area. He was saddened about the slaughter of innocent animals so he went to the court and met the Muslim ruler to explain the significance of nonviolence. He said that cows give us milk so they are like our mother. He said that bulls help to plow fields to produce food grains so they are like our father. Killing these cows and bulls to eat meat is like killing our mother and father and eating their meat. The Muslim ruler was convinced by Mahaprabhu's argument and ordered no more killing of cows and bulls and became an ardent practitioner of nonviolence. Mahaprabhu also converted many criminals and dangerous bandits of his time into great devotees of the Lord. They became compassionate beings. His way of nonviolence attracted thousands of followers.

In modern times, Mahatma Gandhi has been the greatest advocate of the principle of nonviolence. His nonviolent methods made him the leader of the freedom movement in India. He has influenced and inspired many great world leaders. He used nonviolence as a weapon to overthrow British rule, social injustice, and the fight against exploitation. According to Gandhi, equanimity towards all living beings is *ahimsa*—and in this we recognize his debt to classic Hindu thought and to ascetic traditions. He expounded a comprehensive philosophy of nonviolence. He tried to apply nonviolence in *every* walk of life: domestic, institutional, economic, and political. He was unique in extending nonviolence to the domain of economics, thus introducing moral values as a regulating factor in international commerce (Tahtinen 1976, 118, 123).

According to Gandhi, even criminals, whose crimes are a disease in need of a cure, must be treated with nonviolent methods and regarded as our brothers. Prisons should be used as institutions of reform and not as places of punishment (*Ahimsa* 124). For Gandhi, *ahimsa* meant a transformation of the heart that would result in the freedom of his country and the creation of a casteless society. Gandhi wrote:

> Violence is not of the very essence of human nature. One thing we can learn from history is that if war cannot be abolished, there is absolutely no hope for the future of the human race, as sooner or later society is bound to annihilate itself. The reason is quite clear: The advancement of scientific technology and the life destroying power of the nations are increasing. If war is not soon avoided or abolished, a conflict will arise in which entire nations and races will be completely blotted out of existence and even vast continents will be reduced to impotency and dissolution. One thing is clear, therefore; war must be abolished at all costs, if civilization is to survive. Then the madness of violence must be recognized, its causes removed, and its implements destroyed. But how can it be done? It can be done by one means only: the manifestation of a better spirit. It is a change of character and conduct through a change of ideas, reason, and good will—these are the only agencies in a civilized age for effecting such changes. (Gandhi 1948-49)

CONCLUSION

Human conflicts continue to arise. Animals are sacrificed in the name of science and economy. Trees and plants are destroyed in the name of progress. Land is poisoned by using various pesticides, chemicals, and fertilizers, thus endangering the entire food chain.

83

Great rivers and oceans are polluted by chemical wastes. Nuclear tests are killing hundreds of water animals and other life forms. At this juncture, the need for a comprehensive sense of nonviolence has become more pressing than ever before.

The Hindu concept of the spiritual unity of all existence—the Vedantic notion that all things share a fundamental sameness—may work as a basis for establishing a new world peace and may contribute to the long elusive goal of a unity among all humanity.

BIBLIOGRAPHY

Works in English:

Bose, N. K. *My Days with Gandhi.* Calcutta: Nishana, 1953.

Bose, N. K. *Selections from Gandhi.* Ahmedabad: Navajivan Publishing House, 1948.

Chapple, Christopher Key. *Nonviolence to Animals, Earth, and Self in Asian Traditions.* Albany: State University of New York, 1993.

Gandhi M. K. *Nonviolence in Peace and War.* Vol. 1 and 2. Ahmendabad: Navajivan Publishing House, 1948-1949.

Koshelya Walli. *The Conception of Ahimsa in Indian Thought.* Varanasi: Bharatamanisha, 1974.

Shastri, Y. S. *A Collection of Prayers.* Ahmedabad: Yogeshwar Parkashan, 1994.

Tahtinen, Unto. Ahimsa: *Nonviolence in Indian Tradition.* London: Ryder, 1976.

Works in Sanskrit:

Agnipurana. Ed. Khemaraj. Bombay: Shrikishan Dass, n.d.

Astadasasmrtayah. Bombay: Gujarat Printing Press, 1981 V.S.

Atharvaveda. Trans. M. Bloomfield. Oxford: Oxford University Press, 1897.

Bhagavadgita. Trans. J. Goyandaka. Gorakhpur: Gita Press, 1969.

Isadidasopanisad. Delhi: Motilal Baharasi Dass, 1964.

Ishavasya Upanishad. Trans. Swami Chinmayananda. Bombay: Central Chinmaya Mission Trust, 1992.

Mahabharata. Shantiparva and Anusasanaparva. Poona: Bhandarkar Oriental Research Institute, 1932.

Manusmrti. Ed. Pandya Pranajivan Harihar. Bombay: Gujarat Printing Press, 1886.

Ramayana. Ed. J. Goyandaka. Gorakhpur: Gita Press, 1943.

Rgveda. Trans. R. T. H. Griffith. Delhi: Motilal Banarass Dass, 1973.

Chapter 5

INDIGENOUS TRADITIONS OF PEACE: AN INTERVIEW WITH LAWRENCE HART, CHEYENNE PEACE CHIEF

By Daniel L. Smith-Christopher

INTRODUCTION

In discussions of the religious basis for peace and nonviolence, it is rarely the case that indigenous religious traditions within national borders are mentioned, yet many of these religious traditions have a great wealth of traditional teaching about peace, which often include rituals, practices, and teachings that honor peace and values of nonviolence.

These important traditions among indigenous peoples around the world can be cited totally apart from the influences of missionizing traditions such as Islam and Christianity. Many indigenous traditions taught the values of nonviolence and peacemaking for centuries before the arrival of Islamic or Christian missionaries. In some of these societies, for example, violence is virtually unknown (Montagu 1978), while in other societies, the value of nonviolence and/or peace is honored and considered an ideal goal even in the midst of societies that also practice violence (Bohannan 1967; Mead 1937; Augsburger 1992). In other cases, some of the indigenous religious traditions have combined with Christianity or Islam to form a unique, culturally-nuanced expression of that larger world tradition. An obvious frontier in peace research would not only be the traditions of peacemaking in various indigenous societies, but the relationship of those traditions to the arrival of Christianity, Islam, and other transnational religious traditions (Hefner 1993).

In contemporary indigenous societies around the world, the persistence of peacemaking traditions gives voice to the *religious hope* of "subverting hatred." In some small and localized groups, perceptions of holiness and religious values have led many people to stand against the practice of warfare within their traditions. In some cases, these values have led members of these indigenous traditions to carry their values of peacemaking into dialogue with wider societies. One thinks, for example, of the Southwestern American Hopi nation, many of whom declared status as conscientious objectors during American conflicts on the basis of the nonviolent ethos of Hopi tradition (a story that has yet to be fully explored, incidentally). Note, as an example of combined indigenous/Christian traditions, the Mexican group known as "Los Abejos" (The "Bees"). They have engaged in a consciously chosen nonviolent campaign in Chiapas against Mexican military excesses. Further, in Australia it is often noted that violent confrontation against Western settlers in Australia by the Aboriginal Australians is generally absent. Ironically, this lack of violence is dismissed as the result of weakness or explained as some kind of realization by Aboriginals that Western settlement is inevitable. What we need instead is a studied appreciation of many Aboriginal Australian cultures which have sophisticated ethics against interpersonal violence and/or long established ritual forms of conflict resolution that are preferred to confrontational violence.

What follows is one important example of an indigenous tradition of peacemaking. It might well serve as an invitation to additional studies of indigenous traditions.

Lawrence Hart is one of the four "Principal Chiefs" (that is, one of four chosen from 40 Chiefs of the Nation) of the Southern Cheyenne. He is also the Executive Director of the Cheyenne Cultural Center in his home town of Clinton, Oklahoma, in the United States. Lawrence Hart has been actively involved in cultural, economic, and religious rights issues far beyond the confines of his own Cheyenne nation and currently also serves on the Review Committee of the Native American Graves Protection and Repatriation Act, a national advisory body. This interview was conducted for *Subverting Hatred* in the summer of 1998.

INTERVIEW

Can you please describe your culture's ideas about peace? Do you have specific ceremonies that are dedicated to making peace between enemies? Can you describe them?

Hart: We have a council of 44 peace chiefs that was instituted by Sweet Medicine, our culture's hero. There are two legends about the council. The first is about a woman who had a vision or dream (some say it was influenced by her visiting another tribe) and in that vision she suggested that the Cheyenne organize a council of chiefs. There would be 10 men chosen from four societies, and from within that 40, four would be selected as the principal chiefs. Then the four that were chosen as principal chiefs would be replaced with additional men from the societies so the total would be 44.

The other legend is that Sweet Medicine instituted this council. Even if he did not, he gave a lot of instructions about how the chiefs were to live their lives and how they were to be peace chiefs. Sweet Medicine told them that they were essentially to be peacemakers. They were not to engage in any quarrels within the tribe regardless of whether their families or children were involved. They were not to engage themselves in any force or violence, even if their son was killed right in front of their tee-pee. *You are to do nothing but take your pipe and smoke.* There are many other such instructions, but that is the primary one.

There are other aspects to this commitment—such as, if you see your wife of children harmed by anyone, you do not take revenge. Being a chief actually is a way of life. A chief already has generally proven himself in terms of courage or valor when he is selected from within the four societies. Currently, these four societies are the Elk Soldiers, Bow Strings, Dog Soldiers, and Kit Fox. When men are selected from within these societies, they must make a complete break, a complete reversal of who they are. Once they were warriors, but, when they are selected, they become peace chiefs. They are inducted through a ceremony with many rituals. They no longer use force or violence. The families of the chiefs are held almost to that same standard. It's wise that before someone becomes a chief they clear it with the family as well as extended family. Some refuse this opportunity to be a chief.

There are other aspects to this commitment, too. For example, the chief's home becomes a kind of sanctuary, even in contemporary times. Tribal members can go to the chief's home and be safe. No one should be bothered there. Finally, one of the more traditional ways of practicing nonviolence is for the chiefs to meet together in making peace—to ultimately have the ritual of smoking a pipe together with the adversary.

Do you have any sacred traditions, stories, or artifacts that your culture values that somehow speak of traditions of peace?

Hart: The main symbol, of course, is the pipe that is carried by the chiefs, especially the four principal chiefs. Sweet Medicine also gave to the Cheyenne four sacred arrows: two are for the enemy, two are for food. So that means, even though we have peace traditions, we also have warrior societies who protect the tribe.

Have there been debates among your people about the use of violence in gaining equal rights and justice? How do you feel about these debates? How do you think people in your cultural and religious tradition(s) would feel, for example, about Gandhian methods of nonviolent activism? Do you have similar traditions or ideals in your religious tradition?

Hart: When I work for human rights, I would not use force or violence. I believe that nonviolence is generally the stance that the chiefs would take. The Cheyenne would understand that this kind of activism was conducted by some of our peace chiefs in the 1860s when there was a lot of violence on the high plains. In one instance, the chiefs recommended that they sit down and discuss peace with Colorado territorial Governor Evans and his militia. These talks took place at Camp Weld near Denver in September of 1864. The Cheyenne chiefs were very serious about the peace overtures they were making, but as soon as they left, according to the records, Colonel John M. Chivington and Governor Evans began to plot against the Cheyenne. Their attack occurred two months later, on November 29, at Sand Creek where many of these same peace chiefs were camped. There ensued what is known as the Sand Creek Massacre.

What we really don't do is engage ourselves in any kind of activity for human rights as chiefs directly, in the sense of being activists. We certainly work for justice issues, but not traditionally as "activists." Although, for myself, I appreciate Gandhi and Martin Luther King Jr., we do not actively engage ourselves in nonviolent activities.

Do you think your nonviolent beliefs are shared by most of the people in your tradition or are you in a minority among your own people?

Hart: I think we're certainly not in the majority. Nonviolent members are in the minority, but at the same time, I think we're appreciated, especially by those who know this tradition. You should know that in our history, sometimes the peace chiefs have had to stand against our own warriors who believed that war was the best action to take in given circumstances. It is frequently expected—and often did happen—that the chiefs would oppose their own warriors.

Do the teachings about peace in your tradition actually suggest practical steps in making peace? Do you think these teachings have wider political significance?

Hart: Oh yes. The chiefs mediate disputes. The chiefs don't take sides. I think these ideas have the potential for wider application, but it's sometimes very difficult. One of the things that we see today, especially in activities that involve the total community like powwows or special dances, is that there is a lot of patriotism exhibited in many ways. Veterans are highly honored among the Cheyenne. Many people say that's an irony for me as a peace chief. Furthermore, we Cheyenne have our own flag song and many people say, "Its our national anthem." We have alongside this a tradition of being peacemakers. I myself am very conscious of this kind of patriotism that is exhibited especially with other tribes. These tribes highly influence our own, and sometimes they have no such strong peace tradition like our own.

One way in which our young men, and now young women, gain recognition and status is to go into the military and make some kind of achievement. When they do, they are recognized and honored. At the same time, in many of our other more traditional dances held around the local communities, the very first dance is always for the chiefs, that is, the peacemakers. So we have many ironies that occur within our culture.

Generally, a chief also is a servant of the people, not a leader as much as a servant. Not only is he a peacemaker, but he is also expected to help people in ways that he can, and in this kind of servant stance, chiefs are generally recognized last. For example, they are the last to be served at a meal when there is a community gathering (and such gatherings always involve a large meal). Everyone is fed first and the chiefs are fed last. And if they get nothing to eat, that's okay, then the children and especially the elders have been fed first. Then usually right after the meal there will be a dance. And in that dance, chiefs are given recognition. Then, the chiefs are recognized first. It's basically the only time they're recognized first. They are given that kind of esteem, that kind of recognition by the community for who they are.

Please choose two "heroes" or "heroines" from your tradition—one recent (perhaps still living) and one in history. These two persons should be people who, in your mind, best represent your culture's striving for peace. Please tell us about them and what you think their most important message of peace is for us.

Hart: I have many role models. My favorite is White Antelope. He was a chief who was prominent in the 1850s to 1860s and was killed at Sand Creek. He was one of the chiefs who went to the council at Camp Weld with territorial Governor Evans. On the morning of the attack, he had apparently risen early and had gone out away from his village just a bit. When he saw the troops on the horizon he thought that they knew that the Cheyenne were at peace, especially consequent to the peace council at Camp Weld. Even when the charge was sounded for the troops to attack the village, he thought it was a mistake and ran forward toward them and tried to stop them. When he saw that it was a deliberate attack and not a mistake, he stopped and stood there and began to sing his death song. And he continued to stand there, totally unarmed, and sang until he was shot down. I have many such role models, but that's my favorite.

My own grandfather was John Peak Hart, and he was a more contemporary peace maker. He made peace with the Mountain Ute in Colorado. At one time a century ago, the Mountain Utes were our enemies. It was John Peak Hart, as he was known by the Mountain Utes, who created a friendship with them. In that sense he was active in making peace with a tribe that had been our traditional enemies. I was just a small child, in pre-school years, when I would go with him each summer when he traveled to Colorado. Many times today, when I'm in the Four Corners area, whether it's with the Mountain Utes or Navajo, when I say I'm a grandson of John Peak Hart, they tell me he is well remembered by them.

I need to mention a woman because I have an appreciation for many of the women in our tradition. There is one—I know her Cheyenne name—but her first name was Pamela and her last name was "Stands-in-Sight," so Pamela Stands-in-Sight. She's been gone probably 15 years now, but I got to know her and she was a really beautiful person. She was the daughter of a chief who became the wife of a chief, the mother of a chief, and then the grandmother and great grandmother of a chief. And that's unusual. I don't think that's mentioned anywhere among our people.

What do you think are the greatest gifts that your culture can offer the rest of the world? Is there a specific wisdom about peace that you think the rest of the world would benefit from?

Hart: I think to live the kind of life a Cheyenne chief lives is one such contribution we could offer. In fact, there is an expression in our language—I'll say it in Cheyenne "E-ve-hon-e-wo-stane-hev." Translated, it means that person is "living the life of a chief." It's a high compliment and generally would be given to one who is a peacemaker. I think that if people in the world could have lives like that—to emulate the Cheyenne chiefs—then that would be a great contribution.

Remember that this book is also for students and scholars who are interested in studying the issues of peace and religion more carefully. In your opinion, what are the most important issues related to your religious and cultural tradition that are in need of further study? What are the most important un-studied issues with regard to nonviolence and peacemaking?

Hart: I think generally when people hear the word "Indian" they begin to immediately conceive of typical stereotypes, including the one perpetuated by Hollywood and television in its early days. Indians were, and sometimes still are, portrayed as war-like and cruel, and often they were the villains. I think people need to "unlearn" that stereotype. And they can do it by engaging in studies of the peace traditions within different tribal groups. The Cheyenne aren't the only nation who have important peacemaking traditions—there are others, but I think more needs to be published about them. The Navajo, for example, have peacemakers, and the Iroquois nations had a peace tradition.

I'm not sure, though, that one could really get at the heart of our traditions without actually experiencing them. You know, you can study and you can read and hear our traditions, but somehow I think you have to just simply live it in order to gain a full under-standing of it. This is because, along with the traditions, there is a high degree of spirituality associated with everything we do as chiefs. There are many rituals that we use whenever we gather together that are enriching. When we talk about some of these rituals, they sound mundane. But it's just indescribable what happens when we perform them. Traditionally, we gather in a teepee. We never gather anywhere else when the chiefs get together. One of the first things we do is use just a plain bucket of water with a dipper. The bucket might be three-quarters full of water and, in a special ritual, that water is blessed by one of the chiefs who has the authority to do that. I don't have that authority myself, but there are others who do. Then the water is passed from one person to another around the circle and each takes a dipper of water and drinks it until every-one is served that water. Everyone has participated in that ritual of taking water.

When we gather together like that, we have generally gathered from different communities where we live, or different jobs we might have. We've come with a certain amount of "baggage" and there may be some things that are preoccupying our minds, but when we go through this ritual, even as simple as it is, it tends to unite us so that we can think—ultimately think with one mind, one heart. Now the Iroquois have their own rituals. They verbally say "Let us combine our hearts and minds together" after a series of statements, but in our case we take this water and it has the same effect, it combines our heart and mind, and when we talk about a major issue everyone has a right to talk. No one is interrupted, and we talk around the circle until we are finished talking about that issue. We can either move on or continue to talk about that issue.

There are other such rituals that have a very high degree of spirituality. What I want to say is that you can read about it, you can almost visualize what I've just described, but then, you really need to experience it. What I want to say is, as good as literature is, as good as books are, there is a limitation. One can grasp a good understanding of our tradition, one can be influenced by it, by experiencing this kind of life.

RECOMMENDED READINGS

Hart: One of the books that I appreciate very much is *The Peace Chiefs of the Cheyenne* by Stan Hoig (Norman: University of Oklahoma Press, 1980). He has another important book on the Sand Creek Massacre (*The Sand Creek Massacre*, Norman: University of Oklahoma Press, 1961) which gives a good perspective of what happened there. He's a good author, a contemporary author. There are good studies by Peter J. Powell, especially his two-volume series called *Sweet Medicine* (Norman: University of Oklahoma Press, 1969), and another two-volume set entitled *People of the Sacred Mountain* (San Francisco: Harper and Row, 1979). This series is about our sacred mountain, which is Bear Butte in South Dakota. Another author whom I really appreciate is Donald J. Berthrong, whose most recent book is entitled *The Cheyenne and the Arapaho Ordeal* (Norman: University of Oklahoma Press, 1976).

I don't think one should overlook George Bird Grinnell's books, such as *The Fighting Cheyenne* (Norman: University of Oklahoma Press, 1976) and *The Cheyenne: Indian New Heaven* (New Haven: Yale University Press, 1923). Those are good books. There's still another one by Karl N. Llewellyn and F. Adamson Hoebel called *The Cheyenne Way* (Norman: University of Oklahoma Press, 1941). Llewellyn and Hoebel's book is a very scholarly work published in 1941 and it has to do with Cheyenne jurisprudence. It has many accounts of the Cheyenne as peacemakers.

BIBLIOGRAPHY

Augsburger, David W. *Conflict Mediation Across Cultures: Pathways and Patterns.* Louisville: Westminster/John Knox Press, 1992.

Bohannan, P., ed. *Law and Warfare.* Garden City: Natural History Press, 1967.

Hefner, R.W., ed. *Conversion to Christianity: Historical and Anthropological Perspectives on a Great Transformation*. Berkeley and Los Angeles: University of California Press, 1993.

Mead, M., ed. *Cooperation and Competition Among Primitive Peoples*. Boston: Beacon Press, 1937.

Montagu, A., ed. *Learning Non-Aggression*. Oxford: Oxford University Press, 1978.

Chapter 6

NONVIOLENCE IN ISLAM: THE ALTERNATIVE COMMUNITY TRADITION

By Rabia Terri Harris

How should you not fight for the cause of God and of the feeble among men and of women and the children who are crying: Our Lord! Bring us forth from out of this town of which the people are oppressors! Oh, give us from Your presence some protecting friend! Oh, give us from Your presence some defender!

Qur'an, Surah Baqarah

You have not been sent save as a mercy to the worlds.

Qur'an, Surah Anbiya'

Islam is rarely associated with nonviolence in the public mind. The fear that medieval Christendom felt at the swift and broad expansion of Dar al-Islam, the "House of Islam"—with its formidable and vigorous competing culture—is echoed in the fear that modern Westerners often feel at the appearance of Muslims in contemporary conflicts. This negative mindset also dominates the news: the enemy is depicted as clutching a Damascene dagger between his teeth. Seldom acknowledged is another face of Islam, the face turned away from Europe—for the Islamic religion spread throughout Southeast Asia and Africa by way of merchants and teachers, without any military involvement at all.

Islam makes no distinction between "church" and "state." There is scarcely any such entity as an Islamic church, and an Islamic state

RABIA TERRI HARRIS is founder and coordinator of the Muslim Peace Fellowship (MPF), the only organization presently devoted to the consideration and development of Islamic nonviolence. MPF is an associate of the Fellowship of Reconciliation, the oldest and largest interfaith peace and justice group in the United States. Harris, who embraced Islam in 1978, has translated a number of classic works on Islamic spirituality, including Ibn'Arabi's *Journey to the Lord of Power* (Inner Traditions International, Rochester, Vermont, 1981-1989) and Qushayri's *Risalah* (extracts published as *Sufi Book of Spiritual Ascent*, Kazi Publications, Chicago, 1997; full text in press). She is a member of the Jerrahi Order of America.

has always been a controversial institution. This means that Islam makes no distinction between the affairs of this world and those of the next, seeing them as a seamless unity—a reflection of the unity of God. One of the objectives of Muslim life is to make this unity a real experience for human beings. And one of the major obstacles to the human experience of a unity of faith and life is the presence of injustice.

Say: My lord has commanded justice. (Qur'an, Surah A'raf, 29)

The establishment of justice, the Prophet taught us, requires ceaseless activity. The name for this activity is "jihad." The work of nonviolence is the ultimate root of jihad.

THE PROPHET'S JIHAD

The word "jihad" does not mean holy war. Jihad means struggle, or effort. On the basis of a famous hadith of the Holy Prophet,[1] it is traditionally divided into *al-jihad al-akbar*, the Greater Struggle—the inward effort of confronting our lower nature—and *al-jihad al-asghar*, the Lesser Struggle—the outward effort of confronting social injustice. This lesser struggle is not all of one kind, but of many. It includes teaching, and the active pursuit of a culture of peace, as well as resistance to oppression.[2] Where jihad does refer to resistance to oppression, it is also not all of one kind, but embraces both armed and unarmed forms of struggle.

The Holy Prophet engaged in both forms of struggle. This fact is of key significance, for the practice of the Prophet—the Sunnah—stands immediately next to the Qur'anic revelation as a definitive guide for Muslims in every dimension of life. The Qur'an recommended the Prophet to us as "a beautiful example" (Surah Ahzab, 21), and ordered him to say to his community: "If you love God, follow me. God will love you and forgive your sins" (Surah Al-I 'Imran, 31). In consequence, as Schimmel writes:

> In war and peace, at home and in the world, in the religious sphere as in every phase of working and acting, the Prophet is the ideal model of moral perfection. Whatever he did remains exemplary for his followers. (Schimmel 1985, 54)

If the Prophet engaged in armed struggle, therefore, it is clearly permissible and approved by God that Muslims should engage in armed struggle. But the question remains: Under what circumstances?

There is no license in Islam for any war (indeed, for any human enterprise) that falls outside the bounds of the divine commandments and Prophetic practice. Yet there may be fundamental disagreements about how the necessary analogies between these principles and current situations are to be drawn:

> ... differences in the interpretation of the Prophet's sociopolitical activities can easily arise. The material at our disposal is many-sided and often contradictory, and the very history of early Islam poses numerous problems for the faithful as to how to implement the Prophet's ideals. Herein lies one reason for the difficulties that modern nations face when they attempt to create a truly "Islamic" state based on the teachings of the Koran and the Prophetic sunna. (Schimmel 1985, 54)

As we shall see, it is not only modern nations that have faced these difficulties. Such difficulties have formed a painful problem for the Muslim community from the very beginning. The same "beautiful example" which inspired the great heroes of nonviolence in Islamic history was also appealed to for justification by the fiercest opponents of these advocates of nonviolence.

To understand the problems of interpreting the Islamic tradition and applying this tradition to contemporary political issues (as well as critiquing some of these), we must consider how Muslims view the course of the life of our Prophet and also reexamine what we know of the role of the "lesser struggle" against social injustice in it.

THE LIFE OF THE PROPHET

The life of the Prophet of Islam is an extraordinary story and needs an extended format to do it any justice. The subject has inspired hundreds of volumes of narrative, documentation, and commentary. We can sketch only the briefest and most inadequate of outlines here.

The prophetic career of Muhammad, the Messenger of Allah (peace and blessings be upon him),[3] fell roughly into two parts, each with its own great theme. His first task was to persist with unwavering endurance in the face of an increasingly bitter communal repression. This drama unfolded in the Prophet's home city of Mecca, where he began at the age of 40 to receive revelations and to call people to the way of God. At this time he drew to himself a

growing handful of staunch and committed souls. Soon that handful was strong enough to threaten the Meccan elite with a vision of
their own economic demise by means of a social and spiritual revolution. This elite group did their utmost to prevent such an out-
come. The early Muslims resisted the ensuing assaults with legendary courage.[4]

After 12 years of nonviolent resistance, the tide of events turned.
A new challenge, and the demands of a new kind of patience, opened
a second stage in the Prophet's career. The citizens of Yathrib, an
oasis town rife with tribal bloodshed that was situated 200 miles to
the north of Mecca, were impressed by Muhammad's (s) probity
and invited him to relocate as a disinterested arbiter among them.
The Muslim community quietly shifted from Mecca to what came
to be known as Medina and 622 C.E. became Year One of the Islamic calendar.

With the relocation, the persecution of a local minority became
an open war between contending towns—towns with radically different social systems. This state of affairs continued for eight peril-
ous years, yet the Muslim community continued to grow. In 630
C.E. the Muslims gained the victory when they captured the city of
Mecca *without* bloodshed.[5] The entire city adopted the religion of
its peaceful conqueror. All tribal claims to vengeance among Muslims—old or new—were formally abolished. This did not, however, mean an end to all the fighting. The Prophet hoped to extend
Pax Islamica throughout the Arabian peninsula and as far beyond
as God willed. When the Muslims won—and they continued to
win—they offered to Christians and Jews a religiously-protected
status and to different groups of pagan Bedouin a number of different choices from simple truce to adoption by the community. (The
Bedouin eventually universally converted, at least in name.) War
inside the community was forbidden for all (Hourani 1991, 19).

Three years after the conversion of Mecca to Islam, the Messenger who had brought about this social miracle left this world. But
the ripples of his message continued to spread. People came into
Islam by choice and not by force. Contrary to lingering medieval
propaganda, conversion by force is and always has been rigorously
prohibited by Islam. People made the decision to convert not only
because of the positive impression they received of the carriers of

the message, but also probably because they saw Islam as the wave of the future.

Yet the curious relationship between the Way of Peace (for that is what "Islam" means)[6] and the military exploits of its promoters remained ambiguous and troubling. Within a scant few decades after the Prophet's passing, that ambiguity built to its first terrible crisis. The crisis continues to recur.

THREE LOST CAUSES

(1) In the year 680 C.E., just 48 years after the Holy Prophet had gone to meet his Lord—leaving his community to face the temptations of victory without him—a small band of men, women, and children walked into the deserts of Iraq. They were not armed for war. Their leader, al-Husayn ibn ʿAli (r), had received a letter from the people of the city of Kufa. The letter implored him to come to the people's aid against the powerful new rulers of the young Islamic state, rulers whom they perceived to be unjust. Al-Husayn (r) was a grandson of the Prophet and an heir to his revered grandfather's courage, charisma, moral stature, and sense of responsibility. He gathered his family and friends about him and they all came together to answer the Kufans' call.

It appears, however, that the Kufans panicked. Before al-Husayn's party was anywhere near their city, the Kufans fled to the side of their enemies, the officers of the reigning government, raising an alarm against the ally whom they had themselves summoned. The band of 72 peaceful members of the family of the Prophet found itself surrounded by more than a thousand heavily armed soldiers of the nervous Islamic state. For three days under the desert sun the soldiers prevented all access to food and water for al-Husayn's party. And then, according to tradition, when the tiny group of state enemies was "sufficiently weakened," the soldiers slaughtered them all, down to the last infant child (see Schimmel 1986). The incident became notorious as the Massacre at Karbala.

Al-Husayn (r) is known in Islamic tradition as the Prince of Martyrs. There is every indication that he, like the other members of his party, understood exactly what the dangers were and what his fate was likely to be. That did not stop him. He was motivated by something that Gandhi has taught the twentieth century to call *satyagraha*—"soul force." In those days it was known under its more universal name of faith. And the best work of faith, as the Prophet had said, is "to speak a word of truth to an unjust ruler." (*Sunan Abu Dawud* 4330)

The Prince of Martyrs died willingly in pursuit of the best work of faith. While the prospect of his death had not stopped him from proceeding, it stopped Islamic history in its tracks. The Massacre at Karbala horrified the Muslim world, religiously delegitimized the early state's authority, made irrevocable the great sectarian schism of Sunni and Shi'i Islam, and sowed a seed of conscientious opposition to power deep into the fertile ground of the Muslim spiritual tradition.

In the short run, however, the massacre consolidated the control of the ruling 'Umayyad forces. God did not grant worldly victory to the party of al-Husayn.

(2) In the year 922 C.E., another man named Husayn—the profound mystic and widely loved spiritual teacher al-Husayn ibn Mansur al-Hallaj (r)—prepared himself to die. He had been held in the dungeons of the Baghdad government for a decade on charges that combined treason and blasphemy. Yet the vizier had only just found the means to maneuver the highest judge in the land into issuing a death sentence for this particular prisoner.

The 'Abbasid government that held al-Hallaj had come to power, some 173 years earlier, on a wave of popular discontent with the corruption of its predecessor. The earlier 'Umayyad dynasty had been overthrown, in part, through the bitter memory of its role in the martyrdom of al-Husayn ibn 'Ali. The following regime was no less corrupt and bloody—but it was much cannier about public relations. The Sunni 'Abbasids had worked hard to be seen as the champions of Islam, and they were so seen. Except, that is, by the Shi'i politicians of the minority opposition, who claimed that their alternative ideas of government, should they gain the very same state power, would infallibly do a better job.

The Sunni rulers rationalized that troubles were divine punishment for people's sins, while the Shi'i argued that troubles were a divine punishment for bad theology. When social and economic hardships and the cry of injustice continued, "God's will" was conveniently invoked by all.

Al-Hallaj upset this nice political calculus. He came out of the world of the Sufis, mystics, and ascetics who viewed themselves as conservators of the "heart-transmission" of the Holy Prophet. The Sufi community of his time was delicately situated and subject to official persecution. The community attempted to preserve itself through the use of obscure, nonconfrontational language and the maintenance of a very low profile. Hallaj scandalized his fellow Sufis by speaking directly to the public at large of the truths of spiritual experience. This not only put them all at risk, it threatened to shake the foundations of society, for if every individual is authorized to seek (and perhaps find) the holy and to appeal directly to divine justice—if "God's will" is with the people—then what justification remains for the existence of any coercive state?

Hallaj, often called Mansur, "The Victorious," (Schimmel's translation, lit. "The Helped") after his father, had no fear of the worst power of the state. He had long spoken of death as an ecstatic union with his divine Beloved. On 26 March 922 C.E. his hands and feet were cut off, he was hanged on the gallows, and then decapitated; his body was burned and its ashes cast into the Tigris. The story goes that he went to his place of execution in chains—but dancing (Massignon 1975; Schimmel 1975, 62-77).

Another terrible martyrdom. Once again, the soul of the community trembled with the resonance of the call to prayer—a resonance that could never be extinguished. Not only have Muslim poets in the great literary languages praised al-Hallaj for more than a millennium as the embodiment of true spiritual love, but in addition:

> Hallaj's name has found its way into the remotest corners of the Islamic world. It can be discovered in the folklore of East Bengal and the Malayan archipelago; it has been used by some Sufi fraternities in their celebrations, and a Tunisian order has an entire litany in honor of the martyr-mystic. Mansur's suffering through "gallows and rope" has become a symbol for the modern progressive writers in India and Pakistan who underwent imprisonment and torture for their ideals like "the victorious" of old. (Schimmel 1975, 77)

But the social movement that "the victorious" might have sparked, and that the `Abbasid power structure so feared, never caught fire. There was no revolution.

(3) What is victory? In the year 1983 C.E., the great Pathan leader and man of God 'Abdul-Ghaffar Khan (r)—known to his people as Badshah Khan, the king of khans, and to those few Westerners who follow South Asian affairs as "the Frontier Gandhi"—resigned himself once again to imprisonment. The nervous government of the young Islamic state of Pakistan, now led by the dictatorial General Zia, could not tolerate that Khan (or indeed any voice of opposition) should be heard in the land. Yet the Movement for Return to Democracy, a coalition of all civilian parties, was nonetheless attempting a widespread nonviolent resistance to his rule.

Khan understood prison well. After all, he had spent the equivalent of one out of every three days of his life there. And in prison he had found his enlightenment:

> As a young boy, I had had violent tendencies; the hot blood of the Pathans was in my veins. But in jail I had nothing to do except read the Qur'an. I read about the Prophet Muhammad in Mecca, about his patience, his suffering, his dedication. I had read it all before, as a child, but now I read it in the light of what I was hearing all around me about Gandhiji's struggle against the British Raj. (Easwaran 1984)

His whole being was devoted to the unarmed struggle against oppression. It was in the first half of the twentieth century that Khan called his notoriously vengeance-prone Pathan countrymen, the inhabitants of the geopolitically crucial northern "gateway to India," to join Gandhi's nonviolent war against British domination:

> I am going to give you such a weapon that the police and the army will not be able to stand against it. It is the weapon of the Prophet, but you are not aware of it. That weapon is patience and righteousness. No power on earth can stand against it. When you go back to your villages, tell your brethren that there is an army of God, and its weapon is patience. Ask your brethren to join the army of God. Endure all hardships. If you exercise patience, victory will be yours. (Easwaren)

To the astonishment of both the Indians and the English, the fiery, honor-obsessed Pathans heeded the summons of their Badshah, who had already won their loyalty through 21 years of ceaseless village-to-village travel in the service of popular awakening and education. They loved him. What is more, his call to a glorious battle in which absolute courage disdained all lesser arms appealed to their sense of reckless grandeur. Pathan men (and some women) were raised for a violent death. And what death could be more splendid than this?

Badshah Khan indeed raised his army of Khudai Khidmatgars, "Servants of God," and trained them with military discipline. His red-shirted nonviolent Muslim soldiers eventually numbered more than a hundred thousand. A great many of them died as martyrs to nonviolence, just as they had anticipated. They were instrumental in winning Indian independence.

But Khan, alone of all the prominent Muslim leaders of his time, had opposed the subsequent partition of India. In July 1947, when the creation of Pakistan became a virtual certainty and a general referendum was announced, he instructed the members of his army not to vote against Frontier inclusion in the new entity: they were instead to abstain. Pathan country consequently became a Pakistani province. And three weeks after Gandhi was assassinated (January 30, 1948), Badshah Khan pledged his sorrowful allegiance to the new separatist state.

His promise of loyalty did not save him. In March he was elected head of the Pakistan People's Party. In June he was imprisoned and the army of Khudai Khidmatgars was brutally suppressed. The Pathans had freed themselves from British domination but, in another bitter irony, they fell under the domination of their brothers in Islam.

It is unclear, as yet, how far Badshah Khan's greatness will shine from his beloved Frontier country. Perhaps his name will come to illuminate the hearts of Muslims as widely as his predecessors' have done. Peculiarly, he is still unknown, for the machinery of state disinformation was turned full-blast against him: many ordinary Pakistanis and Afghans, for instance, believe that he was merely a nationalist agitator and subversive, and that he died a Hindu. But Hallaj, too, was condemned as a magician, a political manipulator, and a deceiver, and the party of al-Husayn was roundly condemned from official pulpits for many years after he was killed. Still, no disinformation has succeeded in concealing the magnificence of their faith. Their fearless integrity has outlived all desperate efforts to manipulate his story.

In and out of Pakistani jails for the four decades after Independence, as he had been in and out of British jails for the preceding three, Badshah Khan never gave up his work. He tirelessly preached the betterment of the Pathan people and Hindu-Muslim unity. But the Movement for Return to Democracy was crushed, and Badshah Khan died in 1988 with none of his goals in sight.

Muslim proponents of nonviolence, therefore, are faced with a dilemma. Muslims know that unarmed resistance to oppression draws the eternal blessing of Allah, reflects His mercy, and manifests a sublime and noble soul. History has not shown us, however, that nonviolence is always a reliable tool for the removal of oppression. The question is, is armed resistance such a tool? Our contemporary experience has not shown that it is. Yet, on the basis of the paradigmatic experience of the Prophet, we are inclined to believe that it must be.

ISLAMIC JUST WAR THEORY

Much of the Qur'an speaks of struggle—the struggle of the inevitable victory of the true over the false, the right over the wrong. Islam, based upon that revelation, is expected to be the religion of winners. Where is our victory now? Somewhere in those few short years between the passing of the Prophet and the murder of al-Husayn (r), the line that divides jihad for human liberation, on the one hand, and conquest for imperial consolidation, on the other hand, began to be hard to see. The Messenger had urged the Muslims to fight for the cause of God. Later leaders could do the same thing, but without necessarily having the same cause in mind. For the original community, God was close, because His Prophet was in their midst. Then, God seemed to become distant and revealed words began to be turned to ideological ends.

The new Islamic empires needed new territories for economic reasons. If conquest could be religiously justified, consciences could be eased. Like America "saving the world for democracy," the Muslims had a mission for the betterment of mankind. And indeed, Muslim governments were generally no worse and frequently markedly better than the forms of government they superseded. (Far too little attention has been given, for instance, to the routine achievement of multi-religious tolerance within Islamically-inspired realms.)

But just as in the American case, a gap developed between the ideals of the statesmen-soldiers and their policies, and between their policies and their practice—a gap it was more comforting to deny.

Most Muslim scholars between the post-Prophetic period and the dawn of the modern era considered the topic of warfare from a legal perspective and assumed that open conflict between realms ruled by Muslims and those ruled by others was simply inevitable. And as the Prophet had won all his contests, the Muslims would assuredly win theirs. Opinion diverged over whether these contests could be provoked, or only accepted. Theoretical arguments centered on such technicalities as whether it was religiously permissible to enter into a treaty with non-Muslims with a term longer than ten years—that is, the length of the Prophet's longest agreement (AbuSulayman 1993).

But despite the constant citation of holy precedent, most of the medieval Muslim theories of war may be read as a rationalization of imperial "facts on the ground." And for some centuries—from the eighth century C.E. into the eighteenth, with a brief break for the Mongol invasion—the "facts on the ground" remained essentially the same. Muslim societies flourished; Muslim armies went from strength to strength. Establishment Muslim theorists in all fields found less and less need for engaging in fresh thinking. As the old American adage says: "If it ain't broke, don't fix it."

With the emergence of the modern era, the insularity of all civilizations collapsed, and all the rules changed. Time-honored rationales that had made culturally dominant victors comfortable in Islamic governments and palaces no longer worked. It was a vastly disorienting shock for Dar al-Islam. In the wake of all the uproar of new defeats, colonization, persecution, and social fragmentation, Muslims have only begun to work out a coherent new position in the world. Nothing seems useful, and nobody is happy. Islamist intellectual A. A. AbuSulayman writes tartly:

> If there exists any one word to describe the crisis of Muslim thought in the field of external affairs today, that word is "irrelevance." The aggressive attitude involved in the classical approach to jihad as militancy is clearly irrelevant today to a people who are weak and backward intellectually, politically, and technologically. (AbuSulayman 1993, 97)

AbuSulayman, together with many contemporary Muslims, is suspicious and impatient in the face of belated and apologetic re-evaluations of Islam as "Peace Above All," for such talk was the resort of those defeated and colonized generations who had to beg for respect and promise to be good:

> The "liberal" approach, which emphasizes thinking in terms of peace, tolerance, and defensiveness, has also proved irrelevant in a world facing ever-increasing struggles for political, social, and economic liberation. For Muslims, whose energies are needed almost exclusively in the struggle against the conditions, both internal and external, that contribute to their human misery, this approach has proved to be no longer tolerable or useful. (AbuSulayman, 97-98)

For many contemporary Islamic just war theorists, there is an essential analogy to be drawn between the suffering Muslim peoples of today and the beleaguered and vulnerable community around the Prophet. These theorists attempt, therefore, to re-analyze the Prophet's successful jihad to find those key political and strategic insights which will once again liberate the oppressed. They hope thus to restore to Islamic nations that life of dignity and meaning which is encapsulated in the phrase "the sovereignty of God."[7]

Unfortunately, this central historical and textual analogy generally fails. Parts of its failure are acknowledged. Everyone recognizes, for instance, that the current community lacks much of a resemblance to the community of the Prophet. But, rather than considering why an inappropriate analogy remains so devilishly attractive as a political formula in the modern era, these theorists undertake strenuous efforts to *make* it fit. Among activists, this may mean pressuring present-day Muslims to more closely approximate the image of those Muslims who were liberated long ago—thus producing real oppression for the sake of an imagined liberation. Or it may mean redefining "the enemy" to signify something the Prophet never would have allowed. The Prophet, for example, instructed his fighting men that they must never kill old men, women, children, or anybody who merely uttered the phrase, "there is no god but God," or "I give myself up to God"—no matter what the provocation. (e.g., Mishkat al Masibih 838)

Turning to God for the sake of sovereignty and power is different from turning to God for the sake of God. Do religiously inspired political activists genuinely seek liberation and godliness, as the Prophet did, or do they only seek a release from humiliation and a return to empire? Perhaps they themselves are not sure.

The departure of some modern Islamists from the narrow legal formulations of classical theory represents, in itself, a major (and still contested) intellectual revolution. But it is a revolution that has not yet gone far enough. Many Islamists are still attempting to force the similarity of historical contexts and situations, rather than to derive fundamental principles. Consequently, their theories often have wholly neglected the important area of motive. Yet the Prophet gave great importance to motive. He warned us that all acts have the value of their intentions: God, from whom victory is sought, reads the thoughts of the heart. We tell ourselves we seek justice and the Way of God. That claim will be evaluated in the Scales of God—scales whose calibration is fine. Abu Hurayrah reported that the Prophet said:

> The first man (whose case) will be decided on the Day of Judgment will be a man who died as a martyr. He will be brought forward, God will make him recount His blessings upon him, and he will recount them. Then God will ask, "And what did you do (for Me)?" He will say, "I fought for You until I died as a martyr." God will say, "You have told a lie. You fought so that you might be called a brave warrior. And you have been so called." Judgment will be pressed against him, and he will be dragged face downward into Hell. (Sahih Muslim 4688)

Whether aspiring champions of religion are motivated by private ego or by that collective manifestation of ego known as empire, the results are likely to be the same.

In their reanalysis, the Islamists have concentrated wholly on the Prophet's tactics, while ignoring his priorities. For him, the social struggle was only the lesser jihad: the critical struggle was within. No matter what techniques he used, *he could not have established justice if he himself had not been just.* As modern Muslim spiritual master M. R. Bawa Muhaiyadeen wrote of this realization:

> Be in the state of God's peacefulness and try to give peace to the world. Be in the state of God's unity and then try to establish unity in the world. When you exist in the state of God's actions and conduct and then speak with Him, that power will speak with you. (Muhaiyaddeen 1987, 39)

As long as the lesser jihad remains severed from the greater, there can be no true understanding of power. The Prophet has clearly taught us that power is not what the ego takes it to be, and that winning is not necessarily a visible satisfaction. Power and victory are with God alone, and God is neither a banner nor an abstraction. Without a wider understanding of power among Muslims that parallels the Prophetic understanding, oppressor will merely succeed oppressor, and the secret of the Prophet's victory will remain a secret.

NONVIOLENCE: RETURN OF THE REPRESSED

> Let there be no compulsion in religion: truth stands out clear from error. Whoever rejects evil and has faith in God has grasped the most trustworthy hand-hold, which never breaks. (Surah Baqarah, 256)

The Prophet's change in tactics between Mecca and Medina may receive several interpretations. The classical approach is based on the notion of abrogation: that later decisions make former decisions obsolete. Thus, unarmed struggle has been superseded by armed struggle, which is now obligatory upon the faithful (within a variety of legally-disputed limits), until Islam is acknowledged everywhere (AbuSulayman, 116-118). Some modern Islamists modify this view to make it situational. In situations of weakness, unarmed struggle is to be preferred. In situations of strength—and given the existence of oppression, not otherwise—armed struggle is to be preferred. The assumption remains that armed struggle is superior, but must wait, for practical reasons, upon the accumulation of sufficient military power (Peters 1996; Hashmi 1996). This view corresponds to what Gandhi termed "the nonviolence of the weak."

The third view is that power only accumulates to people through the unarmed struggle and continues to reside there. Armed struggle is only a branch, which dies if torn from its root—for it is only unarmed struggle that teaches reliance on God. The assumption here is that power, in its essence, is non-coercive. It is only dissipated, never generated, through coercion. From this perspective, power is not a magic trophy to be fought for, but an infinite spiritual resource which infuses into those who abandon their own objectives for the objectives of their Creator. This is its definition in the Qur'an.

> Have you not seen the one who disputed with Abraham concerning his Lord, because Allah had given him worldly dominance? So Abraham said, 'My Lord is the one who causes life and death.' He said, 'I cause life and death.' Abraham said, 'Allah makes the sun rise in the east. Make it rise in the west!' The one without faith was speechless. Allah does not guide tyrannical people. (Surah Baqarah, 258)

> For whoever fears Allah, Allah will provide a way out (of difficulty), and sustain him from (sources) he does not anticipate. Whoever trusts in Allah, Allah is sufficient to him. Allah is the Accomplisher of His purpose, and has established a destiny for everything. (Surah Talaq, 2-3)

> What army shall help you apart from the Beneficent? Those without faith are only deluded. (Surah Mulk, 20)

The Qur'anic definition of power becomes obscured when worldly dominance is ascendant. It comes to the fore when dominance is rejected. The Prophet steadily shunned all trappings of kingship and insisted that he and his followers commit themselves to servanthood. Thus his most serious troubles began in Medina, when worldly dominance began to appear as a possibility for the Muslims. Abu Hurayrah reported that the Prophet said:

> You people will be keen to have the authority of ruling, which will be a thing of regret for you on the Day of Resurrection. What an excellent wet nurse it is, and how bad for weaning! (Bukhari 9:262)

Abu Hurayrah also reported that the Prophet said:

> Those among the people who are the best at this business (ruling) are those who hate it most. (Bukhari 4:699)

WHAT THE SUFIS CAN TEACH US

And thus it is that the Qur'anic definition of power is best preserved among those Muslims who have been most consistent in avoiding the pursuit of worldly dominance: the Sufis. The Sufis are mystics and ascetics. But what are mystics and ascetics? The Sufi enterprise is many-stranded. Like every other lengthy human undertaking, Sufism has had its historical ups and downs, its eras of special concentration upon this theme or that. And among the artifacts of its history are the impressions held by many that Sufism and the rest of Islam are only distantly related; that Sufi interests are wholly interior and neglect the "real world" of human interactions; that Sufi writing is a thicket of impenetrable esoteric arcana and of precious little relevance to the conduct of life. In some circumstances, these impressions are accurate. In others, they are not. In still others, they have been deliberately created. (Hallaj tore that veil, and paid for it with his life. Most Sufis have been more prudent.)

For many Muslims today, Sufism symbolizes the withdrawal from political engagement that led to the collapse of the Muslim empire. To such people, it represents an embarrassment to be suppressed. But by dismissing the Sufi tradition, Muslims lose all access to a vast treasury of insights persistently collected since the Prophetic era, insights which form a vital and necessary complement to the rest of Islamic thought. Only through a particular kind of ignorance could AbuSulayman have written that in classical Islam, "Social sciences, such as political science, psychology, sociology, and social psychology, were absent" (AbuSulayman, 87). These are sciences in which the Sufis specialize. They are simply unnamed and, therefore, go unrecognized by outsiders. It is true that they do not take the form of other Islamic sciences or of Western sciences either: they can't. Islamic social sciences must deal with a conceptually different kind of politics: the politics of what the Qur'an calls power, to which the state is irrelevant, and in which the Greater Jihad comes first. The 'Abbasid empire found this "politics of the greater Jihad" dangerous. Today's Muslims may yet find it indispensable.

Muslim proponents of nonviolence can challenge the world peace community to reconsider its fundamental goal. Is the universal core of nonviolence the quietism which is appropriate to some spiritual traditions, or is it to struggle for justice in a just fashion with the goal that our current opponents might gladly become our future allies?

> The good and the evil are not equal. Repel (evil) with that which is better: then the one between whom and you was enmity shall become like an intimate friend. (Surah Ha Mim, 34)

Muslims in our turn must consider closely whether such a jihad, given the monstrous brutality of modern war, can now be religiously licit or divinely acceptable if it is anything but unarmed. As Bawa Muhaiyadeen writes:

> It is compassion that conquers. It is unity that conquers. It is Allah's good qualities, behavior, and actions that conquer others. It is this state that is called Islam. The sword doesn't conquer; love is sharper than the sword. Love is an exalted, gentle sword. (Muhaiyadeen, 34)

This is old territory in spiritual terms, but an intellectual frontier. Everything is waiting to be done. It is time to put together the pieces, to see the alternative Islamic community tradition as rich with important messages for all of us. It is time for Muslims to reclaim the principle of *no-compulsion*, which the rest of the world calls nonviolence, as our own and to share it with our global community.

SUGGESTED READINGS

AbuSulayman, `AbdulHamid A. *Towards an Islamic Theory of International Relations: New Directions for Methodology and Thought.* Herndon, Va.: International Institute of Islamic Thought, 1993.

Dukrrani, Tehmina. *Edhi: A Mirror to the Blind.* Islamabad, Pakistan: National Bureau of Publications, 1996. Abdul-Sattar Edhi, the great contemporary champion of nonviolence in Pakistan, is wholly committed to the service of the poor. His nature is startlingly fierce and provides an edifying contrast in style to the gentle Badshah Khan.

Easwaran, Eknath. *A Man To Match His Mountains: Badshah Khan, Nonviolent Soldier of Islam.* Petaluma, Calif.: Nilgiri Press, 1984. The only biography of this modern martyr available in the West, it suffers from the biases of its author who, while sympathetic, is more an admirer of Gandhi than a keen observer of Islamic nonviolence. A biography of Badshah Khan that would be genuinely useful to Muslims remains to be written. Easwaran's book should be read in conjunction with Dukrrani.

Esack, Farid. *Qur'an, Liberation, and Pluralism.* Oxford: Oneworld Press, 1997. Esack, an important organizer of resistance to South African apartheid, currently serves as one of that country's Commissioners of Gender Equality. He is also the first Islamic liberation theologian. This book is a groundbreaking example of essential new hermeneutics.

Hashmi, Sohail H. "Interpreting the Islamic Ethics of War and Peace." In *The Ethics of War and Peace*, ed. T. Nardin. Princeton: Princeton University Press, 1996.

Hourani, Albert. *A History of the Arab Peoples.* Cambridge: The Belknap Press of Harvard University, 1991.

Lings, Martin. *Muhammad: His Life According to the Earliest Sources.* Rochester, Vt.: Inner Traditions International, 1983. Any adequate inquiry into any aspect of Islam must be based upon a familiarity with the character and calling of its Prophet. This version of his biography is packed with traditionally transmitted historical details, while successfully conveying a taste of the tremendous impact of his personality and faith.

Massignon, Louis. *The Passion of al-Hallaj, Mystic and Martyr of Islam.* 4 vols. Princeton: Princeton University Press, 1975.

Muhaiyadeen, M. R. Bawa. *Islam and World Peace: Explanations of a Sufi.* Philadelphia: The Fellowship Press, 1987. This long meditation on the topic by a modern Sri Lankan Sufi master contains a wealth of unique insights, as well as key traditional stories and teachings on the achievement of peace.

Peters, Rudolph. *Jihad in Classical and Modern Islam: A Reader.* Princeton: Markus Wiener Publishers, 1996.

Robson, James, trans. *Mishkat al Masabih.* Sh. Muhammad Ashraf, Lahore, 1975.

Satha-Ananad, Chaiwat (Qader Muheiddeen). *The Nonviolent Crescent: Two Essays on Islamic Nonviolence.* Alkmaar, Holland: International Fellowship of Reconciliation, 1996. Qader Muheiddeen of Thailand is one of the few contemporary Muslim scholars devoting himself to the development of nonviolence theory. This monograph contains, along with a case study of a nonviolent Muslim action in Thailand, his influential essay arguing that the indiscriminate nature of modern warfare renders it automatically religiously illicit, or *haram.*

Schimmel, Annemarie. "Karbala and the Imam Husayn in Persian and Indo-Muslim Literature" *Al-Serat* XII (1986).

Schimmel, Annemarie. *And Muhammad Is His Messenger.* Chapel Hill: University of North Carolina Press, 1985.

Schimmel, Annemarie. *Mystical Dimensions of Islam.* Chapel Hill: University of North Carolina Press, 1975.

The curious reader is also referred to *As-Salamu `Alaykum*, the newsletter of the Muslim Peace Fellowship (Box 271, Nyack, New York 10960).

NOTES

[1] Hadith, generally translated as "tradition," is more literally "report," or "news." The hadith literature contains a vast body of accounts of the Prophet's sayings and actions, the majority of which are accompanied by a careful listing of the series of reporters through whom each account was conveyed. Medieval Muslims developed painstaking sciences for weighing the authenticity of such reports: modern Muslims are hesitating on the brink of expanding their predecessors' efforts. The hadiths are second only to the Qur'an as an authoritative source of Islamic teaching. This chapter cites two of the most highly regarded traditional collections, *Sahih Bukhari* and *Sahih Muslim,* but it makes reference to two others, *Mishkat al-Masabih* and *Sunan Abu Dawud.*

[2] A number of hadiths indicate the fluidity of the concept of jihad. For instance, the Prophet's wife `A'ishah (r), when she asked the Prophet whether women should not fight, was told that the best jihad is a properly performed Pilgrimage (Bukhari 4:43). Concerning the Qur'anic verse, "Urge the faithful to strive. If there are 20 steadfast among you, they shall overcome two hundred" (Surah Anfal, 65), an early commentator said, "I see that this verse applies to the commanding of good and the forbidding of evil" (Bukhari 6:175). The Prophet stated, "The one who looks after a widow or a poor person is like a warrior in Allah's cause" (Bukhari 7:265).

[3] It is Islamic custom not to mention the names of the prophets, their companions, or holy people who have passed away without a benediction. The traditional benediction for the name of the Prophet is, in Arabic, *salla Allahu ʿalayhi wa sallam*: "May God bless him and grant him peace." We shall abbreviate it hereafter by (s). The traditional benediction for Companions of the Prophet is *radiya Allahu ʿanhu*: "May God be pleased with him (or her)." We have abbreviated it by (r).

[4] For instance, there is the celebrated story of Bilal (r), a black slave from Abyssinia, whose master staked him out in the midday sun with a huge rock on his chest, vowing that he would stay that way until he renounced the teaching of the Prophet and worshipped the local gods. Bilal endured, repeating "One, One." One of the wealthiest Muslims was able to negotiate his ransom. He was bought and freed and subsequently became the first Caller to Prayer in Islam (Lings, *Muhammad*, 79.)

[5] The events of the capture of Mecca make a case study in the tactics of nonviolence. Two years previously the Muslims had marched toward Mecca in large numbers—but unarmed, for Pilgrimage. The Meccans had felt that they could not fight unarmed pilgrims without inflicting serious damage on their own politically crucial prestige. They also felt that it would be equally disastrous if the Muslims successfully entered their town. They met the Pilgrimage party well outside the sacred precincts, for negotiations. The Prophet, instead of continuing the march, and in circumstances of great tension, made a truce with the Meccans, permitting them to specify conditions unfavorable to the Muslims. His people were dismayed, but he assured them that the treaty constituted a victory.

For two years people of Mecca and Medina talked freely, with the result that the Muslim community doubled in size, and the Muslims were able to consolidate their position in other directions. Then a Meccan ally tribe broke the truce, and the Prophet again marched on the city, this time in arms. However, there was now almost no resistance. Stating that he intended to treat his former enemies as Joseph had treated his brothers, he granted a general amnesty (Lings, 245-256, 297-303).

[6] Literally, Islam means surrender or submission (to the divine will), but both of those words are so semantically loaded in English as to be almost incapable of communicating the real impact of the term. The word derives from the same root as the word for peace—*salam*—and essentially conveys reconciliation with God. Muslims greet each other with greetings of peace; Muslim five-times-daily prayers are regularly concluded with the remembrance, "Our God, Thou art Peace; Peace is from Thee."

[7] Radical Islamist ideologies agree that the work confronting activists is the restoration of divine order. They differ considerably in their understanding of the relation between the divine order and human nature, but tend to give minimal attention to the deep issues surrounding either term.

Chapter 7

"LET YOUR LOVE FOR ME VANQUISH YOUR HATRED FOR HIM": NONVIOLENCE AND MODERN JUDAISM

By Jeremy Milgrom

INTRODUCTION

> For too long has my soul shared space with hatred of peace
> I am peace,[1] but when I speak, they opt for war.
>
> Ps. 120:6-7

One of the greatest sorrows of my spiritual life has been the realization that one can easily make a case, based on Jewish sources, for perpetuating violence. As a former Israeli soldier currently active in the Israeli human rights community, I have seen violence promoted and inflicted from both sides. As a Conservative rabbi trained to participate in the creation of a Jewish public space, I have been burdened with the understanding that the pursuit of the Zionist dream over the last 120 years has been inseparable from violence, thus giving violence widespread local and international Jewish legitimization.

This essay will attempt to stake out the claim for Jewish nonviolence as part of the struggle that I, as an heir to a nineteenth-century Jewish universalist optimism, never thought needed to be fought; it is my prayer that the turn of the millennium heal the spiritual devastation of the twentieth century, most notably (in this context) the return of violence to Jewish consciousness and practice.

JEREMY MILGROM is founder and executive director of Clergy for Peace and associate director of and consultant to Rabbis for Human Rights. He has been director of the Arab/Jewish Project, Hebrew University Hillel, and program director for the Israeli Interfaith Association. Rabbi Milgrom is a fellow of the Shalom Hartman Institute of Advanced Studies, Jerusalem, and a lecturer on the Bible for Congregation Mevakshei Derekh.

JUDAISM AND NATIONALISM

Modern Jewish nationalism, whose roots are ancient, has both engendered and been influenced by European nationalism, and shares its material achievements and moral failures. It is based on a particularism, that is, a narrowed perspective derived from the foundational Israelite covenant in the Bible whose scope was cosmic and intent benign. The interaction between Jews, the biological successors to those Israelites, and the world has been the story of both fruitful reciprocity and a calamitous incompatibility. The ideological descriptions, prescriptions, and visions of this relationship to the world are both negative and positive. We find them in the Bible (written during the first millennium B.C.E.), rabbinic literature of the following millennium, and the subsequent Jewish medieval and modern literature. The story of violence in Judaism that is contained in all these works must be appreciated in order to clear the deck and make room for a fruitful discussion of the nonviolent alternative.

Finally, we cannot proceed further without positing the complex duality of things Jewish. The term "Jewish" has ethnic connotations relating to the Jewish people, as well as spiritual connotations relating to the Jewish religion. Jewish religious teachings will, therefore, be constantly resonating with the situational reality and needs of Jews. Furthermore, the extent to which Judaism can be seen as a global, and not tribal, religion will be determined not only by the weight of Jewish sensitivity to other religions and cultures but also by the ability and desire of non-Jews to appropriate Israel's story as its own.

THE PLACE OF THE BIBLE IN JEWISH CULTURE: THE PEOPLE AND THE BOOK

Mohammed's seventh-century definition of Jews (and Christians) as *ahel al-kitab* (People of the Book) attests to the age-old centrality of the TaNaK (the Hebrew Bible, the "Old Testament" from a Christian perspective) to Judaism. However, the first book that a traditional Jew encounters in daily practice is not the Bible but the prayer book, and the determining texts in religious jurisprudence are, again, not the Bible but the Talmud and medieval law codes. Therefore, while the Bible has played a pivotal role in establishing and devel-

116

oping not only Jewish values and attitudes but also those of the entire western world, in order to appraise the Bible's real impact on Jews today, it would be useful to outline its place in a variety of contemporary Jewish cultures.

For a considerable percentage of the Jewish people, particularly those living in Israel (where Jewish communal life is less likely to be organized around a synagogue than it was during the Diaspora), the Bible is not experienced in a ritual setting but is rather a national literature, a cultural treasure acquired in school, whose relevance is reinforced through constant political indoctrination.[2] Thus, national pastimes, such as hiking and archaeology, are dressed with verses from the Bible containing ancient place names that have been newly restored, providing an alternative system of symbols and rituals that bypass certain features of traditional Jewish religiosity but end up with a similar nationalist orientation with its sacred spaces—a unique form of "civil religion." This appropriation of biblical verse and terminology is a critical aspect of the modern Israeli reality, but since this essay is meant to explore the *religious* sides of Jewish culture, we shift our attention to the presence of the Bible in Jewish ritual.

In the central communal event of the week, three to five chapters of the Torah (the five books of Moses) are liturgically read and studied. This annual liturgical cycle allows the synagogue-going Jewish community to re-experience the Genesis narratives, the enslavement in and exodus from Egypt, and the 40 years of wandering in the desert as well as to re-encounter the chapters of civil and ritual law that provide the raw material for the exposition (*midrash*) of Jewish law (*halachah*). One might argue that the process creates an internalization of the outlook of the biblical historiographer.

Other sections of the Bible are used with differing frequency. Some psalms are incorporated into the statutory daily, weekly, or holiday prayer cycle. A wider selection of psalms finds its way into private devotional use. Some chapters of the prophetic and historical books are attached to the weekly Torah readings as *haftarot*, and other chapters are read on particular holidays. Independent reading of the Bible on its own is relatively rare and, since most of the Bible does not make its way into liturgical use, large sections, aside from the Torah, are a lost resource to most religious Jews, including those who are well-versed in rabbinic texts.

FROM VIOLENCE TO NONVIOLENCE: READING
VIOLENCE IN AND OUT OF JEWISH TEXTS

The regular worshipper in weekly services in which the Torah is read does not encounter a carefully screened, morally acceptable, and pre-selected Sunday School text but rather the full biblical narrative, which at times reads like an x-rated story permeated with the entire range of lamentable human failings. More jarring still are the prescriptive passages, particularly in the Book of Deuteronomy, demanding the physical eradication of idolaters (whether an individual idolater, or a family, a clan, a city, a nation, or a cluster of nations of idolaters) and the decimation of Israel's political enemies (Deut. 7:1-2; 13:2-19; 20:16-17). These commandments of violence posit the existence of a God whose attributes include those of a terrifying, partisan warrior (Ex. 15:3; Deut. 34:29).[3]

Yet, as a pulpit rabbi, I have hardly ever witnessed the revulsion of sensitive congregants because of an encounter with these texts or their subsequent distancing from anything to do with religion. I believe people who leave (or never entered into) synagogue life do so for other reasons. In fact, the atmosphere that pervades every synagogue I have ever attended, or heard of, during the reading of even the most violent of these passages is (thank God) never one of agitation or incitement. It is, instead, something close to the meditative, contemplative, peaceful core of religion. There is obviously something between or beyond the lines of those texts that allows the worshipper to defuse and transcend the unbridled call for violence previously noted.

The prevailing fashion in liberal circles to decry the grave danger in the ritual use of these texts indicates a basic ignorance of the actual dynamic of synagogue life. There is nothing easier than finding scriptural quotations on any subject: All that is required is an ability to read a concordance coupled with a particular bias. The question is: How accurately can any set of verses reflect the beliefs of a culture? At best, culling quotations from old sources can tell us something about an early stage of that culture's development. As difficult as it may be in today's politically polarized world, we will have to drop our prejudices and make an honest effort to enter into the spiritual environment of the devotees of this culture to find out what the quotations in mind really meant—and mean—to the devotees.

For most worshippers, entering the synagogue is a means of escape from the outside world and a search for refuge in a Jewish space. The verbal content of that which is chanted may be of relatively small importance to the worshipper who primarily experiences community. Frequently, when the verbal content is not translated into the vernacular, its actual meaning is partially or totally inaccessible (not a completely undesirable situation, considering some of these texts). In many cases, the normative meaning of a violent commandment or memory has been moderated, spiritualized, allegorized, or deactivated by Jewish tradition. The following fall into this category: divinely inspired wars (*milkhamot mitzvah*) against Canaanites; the war against Amalek; and even animal sacrifice. Receiving the text through this filter, the worshipper is basically deaf to its literal meaning (*pshat*). For attentive and demanding listeners, however, the plain text exists and is incorporated into their lives in sophisticated, albeit ambiguous, ways.

STUDYING IS THE HIGHEST RELIGIOUS PRIORITY

For more than two thousand years, well back into the time of the Second Temple, the focal and dominant Jewish (religious) activity has been *talmud torah*, Torah-related study. Religious leaders have no hierarchical status but are judged on the basis of their proficiency in the texts. The position of authority is the "Rabbi" ("teacher") and the highest accolade is *talmid khachamim*, a student of the sages (plural, *talmidey kkhachamim*).[4]

The subject matter of *talmud torah* began as the application of *torah shebichtav*, the literal Torah, to everyday life. But with the emergence of *torah shehbehalpeh*, derived Torah (the rabbinic law codes of late antiquity and the Middle Ages and their interpretation) the focus of *talmud torah* was shifted away from the five books of Moses to the massive secondary literature. Surprisingly, this huge corpus is not considered to be esoteric or off-limits to all but specialists. About one-third of Israel's Jewish teenagers, those enrolled in religious high schools, spend upwards of five classroom hours a week on these texts, while students of the elite Yeshiva high schools devote much more time to *torah shehbehalpeh* than to secular subjects.[5]

Since political power (and its accompanying need for organized violence) was only a remote possibility during most of the period that *torah shehbehalpeh* was developed, there was no demand to expound or expand on those sections of Torah dealing with violence, and they fell into relative neglect. The energy of the scholars went into more pragmatic concerns, such as the dietary laws and the observance of the Sabbath. While messianic stirrings[6] were not unusual during almost two thousand years of exile (that is, from even before the end of the Jewish political entity in 70 C.E. to the founding of the modern State of Israel, 1948), certain discussions, such as the kind of armaments that would come into use in the battle of Armageddon, were never seen as necessary. In fact, even though the laws having to do with animal sacrifices continued to be studied,[7] it was not so much so that the Temple ritual could be reinstituted, but rather this study served as a kind of psychological denial of the destruction of the Temple (the second Temple having been destroyed in 70 C.E.). Similarly, even though Jews continued to study the laws of capital punishment long after the Sanhedrin had lost authority to execute, there was no attempt to update the technology involved.

Volumes of traditional commentary have been written on a single halachically (legal) or midrashically (exhortatory) interesting chapter of the Torah. This amount of material written on subjects considered to be of serious interest to Jewish life dwarfs the material available for *all* the "troublesome passages" that are the concern of this article. Indeed, the texts that we thought might incite are actually greeted with a certain inattentiveness when they are read in the synagogue.

Yet, the potential for life-threatening applications of violent texts still exists, as does the fear that even if scholars of hatred might be sequestered in halls of study, their teachings could leak to a troubled public and find fertile ground.[8] Zionism is the most significant development in twentieth-century Judaism. The willingness of Zionists "to get one's hands dirty" carries with it, at the very least, the chance that biblical texts of violence will be reactivated. There is clearly a need for developing a methodology of reading these texts that will counter this danger. What follows is one such attempt to wrestle with the story of violence without apologetics or denial and yet to emerge with a nonviolent Torah.[9]

FROM CREATION TO DESTRUCTION: A SYMPATHETIC READING OF TEXTS ON VIOLENCE IN THE BIBLE

Genesis

Before focusing on its main topic, which is the historic interaction between God and Israel, the Bible attempts to provide a theological history of the human race and the world at large. The dream world in which the human story begins (in both its versions, the first and second chapters of Genesis) is hierarchical yet harmonious: God commands and blesses; man is given a mate; in giving woman her name, man dominates her; humans rule and give names to the animals, but do not kill them (Gen. 1:29-30). All are vegetarian.

This hierarchy of man over woman over animals is portentous because it anticipates the first chain reaction of disobedience: the eating of forbidden fruit, whose consequence is a sharpened hierarchy in which domination and hostility are more the rule than the exception (Gen. 3:14-19). Violence enters through the back door: after the banishment from Eden, God posts the Cherubs with "a flashing rotating sword," the first weapon, to keep Adam from re-entering Eden (3:24). God also moves away from primordial intimacy with other creatures as well: having clothed Adam and Eve with animal skins (3:21), God now accepts Abel's animal sacrifice (4:4).

The violence of antediluvian society (Gen. 6:13), precipitated by the murder of Abel and the brutality of Lemech (5), escalated to a deterioration of a higher order. Notice how Lemech testifies to his victimhood (4:23) and uses it as a basis for the privileged degree of revenge that he claims—11 times that of Cain.[10] Lemech, like the serpent in the Fall, echoes God's words, but is actually using them to his own advantage.

The Bible asserts both a human predisposition towards violence and a divine determination to purge the world of violence (Gen. 6:5; 8:21). Alas, God's solution, the flood, is a wholesale destruction of (human) sinners and (plant and animal) innocents in an attempt to wipe out sin (Talmud Bavli, Berachot 10, on Ps. 104:35).[11] The reestablishment of God's covenant with the human race and with the world (9) is a lesson in both repentance and disarmament. God regrets the flood and puts the rainbow in the sky as a promise never again to unleash such devastation.

Sadly, a comparison of the divine order prescribed in Genesis chapters one and nine shows that victory over violence has not yet arrived. Following the institutionalization of animal sacrifice, the dietary laws are revised to allow for the slaughter and eating of animals; violence against humans, by animals as well as by fellow humans, is anticipated and, in the case of murder, capital punishment is sanctioned as well. Far from the harmony and optimism prescribed in the creation story, the postdiluvian world is admittedly imperfect. Jewish tradition sees its role as working towards the repair of the world, *tikkun olam*.

Organized, glorified human violence will not appear again in the Bible until the time of Abraham, the Bible's first war hero (Gen. 14), who is, not coincidentally, also the Nation Builder par excellence (12:2). On this, compare the hassidic tradition attributed to the Rabbi of Apt:

> When God promised to make of Abraham "a great nation," the Evil Urge whispered to him: "'A great nation'—that means power, that means possessions!" But Abraham only laughed at him. "I understand better than you," he said. "'A great nation' means a people that sanctifies the name of God."[12]

This implicit critique of Jewish nationalism has its roots, of course, in the Prophet Samuel's response to the popular demand for the institution of a monarchy (1 Sam. 8).

While this episode of sanitized warfare[13] in Genesis is uncharacteristic of the Patriarchs who looked after their own interests in more subtle ways, there runs a strain of family discord throughout the book of Genesis. The rivalry between brothers (sometimes reflecting the rivalry between wives) reaches its violent peak with the staged murder of Joseph by his brothers (Gen. 37), and the rest of Genesis is an attempt to find a happy end to that cycle of hatred. God acquiesces to Abraham's problematic behavior towards his firstborn, Ishmael, and first initiates and then cancels the divine command that Abraham immolate his second son, Isaac, at the last moment (22). This model of parenting does not continue in the narrative to the very next generations, but will leave its mark in Israeli law and later Jewish history: fathers will invoke the binding of Isaac when they slaughter their children to "save" them from forced conversion by the Crusaders.

Yisrael Yuval analyzes the literary records of medieval martyrdom and shows how fathers slaughtered their children, intending it as an offering based on the texts retelling Abraham's offering of Isaac. These fathers were surely aware of the tradition that claimed that Abraham actually did slaughter his son and that Isaac was resurrected, so that in seeing themselves as Abrahams, called by God to sacrifice their sons, they were also imploring God to intervene and resurrect their children. Yuval's article, and particularly his decision to demythologize the horror of medieval martyrdom, aroused such strong reactions that the Historical Society of Israel, who published his article, devoted a double issue of their journal to the controversy he aroused (Yuval 1993).

While this survey focuses on reading problematic texts of violence, three cases of nonviolent conflict resolution indicate that a basically optimistic attitude toward subverting hatred predominates in the Patriarchal narratives: the division of land between Abraham and Lot (Gen.13); Isaac's successful battle for water (26); and the reconciliation between Jacob and Esau (33). Left to their own devices,[14] the Patriarchs know how to do the right thing and how to distance themselves from violence (e.g., the repeated condemnation by Jacob of the massacre of the Shechemites done by Simeon and Levi) (34:30; 49:5-7).

Analysis

This retelling of the Genesis narrative aims to show the biblical author's desire to color the violence of the tale in a tragic light. Not only is the violence undesirable, it is a tragic development from conditions and patterns of behavior that overpower the protagonists. The most tragic figure in Genesis, and throughout the Bible, is God (attributed to the preeminent Talmudist Saul Lieberman; cf. Muffs 1992, 4, 160). God, far from being an omnipotent Aristotelian unmoved mover, is a model of frailty and regret. The nuanced reading of the text shows us that God seems to have had no choice but to build domination into creation. But we, who see how this ostensibly harmless domination leads to hierarchy and disobedience and finally violence, can take measures to establish the con-

123

ditions of partnership necessary for a nonviolent society. The biblical God is an emotional God with whom we can commiserate when desperate, extreme measures are taken (the flood) and whom we can celebrate when God learns to control his awesome divine power (the rainbow).

EXODUS TO DEUTERONOMY

While God seems to stay in the wings during the Patriarchal saga,[15] particularly in the Joseph story, the Exodus story is one of full-scale divine intervention. The violence of the Ten Plagues has a double purpose: to humble haughty Pharaoh (Ex. 5:2) and to bring him and others—the Egyptians, the Israelites, the entire cosmos (9:16)—to acknowledge God. (The operation is a success but the subject dies and, in the process, Pharaoh becomes a more sympathetic character while the supposedly humble Moses inherits the mantle of pride.) (cf. 7:5; 11:3).

Incidentally, this portrayal of Moses is not the first, or last, case where the Israelite main character is shown in a less favorable light than his pagan protagonist (e.g., Abraham and Pharaoh in Gen. 12, Abraham and Avimelech in Gen. 20, Isaac and Avimelech in Gen. 26, Jacob's sons and the Shechemites in Gen. 34, and Jonah and the sailors in Jon. 1). This portrayal cannot be accidental, considering the Bible's bias against paganism, and is another example of the usefulness of nuanced reading to reveal the internal textual potential for fighting prejudice within the text.

In Exodus, the use of force is more than instrumental: it is of the essence—reality itself is terrifying and humans must realize their total dependence on an omnipotent God whose ways are unknowable.[16] It has been argued, for example, that the drowning of the Egyptians in the Red Sea (whose suffering, incidentally, is mourned at every celebration of the Passover Seder) is not directly necessary for saving Israel physically but rather to strengthen the faith of the Israelites (Ex. 14:31) and thereby ultimately ensure their survival. Elements of this line of reasoning that attempts to deflect the emphasis and meaning away from using the episode as a defense for violence begin already in the Hellenistic period in the work known as Wisdom of Solomon.

God's victory over Egypt is meant to terrify the enemies next in line, the Canaanite nations, so that they flee the incoming Israelites or are decimated.[17] According to the most extreme passage (Deut. 20:16-17), the Israelite army cannot accept the surrender of the indigenous nations; they, like the idolatrous Israelite city (13), fall under a total ban, *kherem*, and *must* be put to death.

Analysis

This latter passage condemning the idolatrous city indicates both the scope and the rationale for this ban and gives us a sword with which we will attempt to cut the Gordian knot of divine or divinely-inspired violence:

> You shall put its inhabitants to the sword, all of them, including their cattle. The booty you should collect outside and burn the city and its booty as a complete offering to God; it shall remain a mound of ruins, never to be rebuilt. Let nothing out of all that comes under the ban be found in your possession, so that God may turn from his anger and show you compassion and be compassionate to you and increase you as he swore to your forefathers, provided that you obey God and keep all God's commandments which I give you this day, doing only what is right in the eyes of the Lord your God. (Deut. 13:16-19)

Typical of the Deuteronomic author is the appeal to Israel's desire for self-preservation, which Israel can only achieve through its maintenance of the covenant with God. Most striking about this passage, however, is the juxtaposition of cruelty and compassion: humans are required to reach unbelievable levels of cruelty in order to receive divine compassion.[18] On the one hand, we find the instrumentality of the Other, that is, the non-Israelites, which we saw in the case of the Exodus, but here the immolation of the idolater is not so much to enhance God's reputation, nor is it a deterrent to Israel's enemies. Rather, the sacrifice seems necessary simply to satisfy God.

Could we possibly get any further from the fundamental biblical postulate basic to religious humanism that, created in God's image, there is a divine spark in every human being that makes the preservation of all human life the highest priority? On the positive side, we find here not only the divine promise of compassion for God's faithful, in harmony with the rest of the divine commandments, but the granting to humans of a power to manipulate God's emotional state that takes God from anger to compassion, a power with cosmic ramifications (an idea that, though marginal in the Bible, is greatly expanded in the mystical tradition of the Kabbala). Rabbinic tradition (Babylonian Talmud Yebamot 79a) sees in the divine promise, "so that God will show you compassion," in the passage cited above the granting to humans of the implicitly divine capacity for compassion ("As God is considered to be merciful, so too, should you be merciful") (Sifre Deut. Ekev. 49). To the rabbis, compassion is part and parcel of the religious life.

While rabbis understood God's capacity for mercy to be limit-less and worthy in principle of human emulation, *imitatio dei*, the rabbis sought to limit the human application of compassion, saying, "One who is kind to the cruel will, in the end, be cruel to the kind" (Kohelet Raba 7:16). But this occasion was not one of those times, and the rabbis indicate that this commandment would never be applied (Tosefta, Sanhedrin 14.1; Bavli, Sanhedrin 71a). And finally, God's dependence on human beings, that is also shown in this passage, gives us a foot in the door in moral decision-making, one which the rabbis exercise in their modification of the application of the *kherem* against the indigenous nations of Canaan.[19]

Modern biblical scholarship holds that the historiography of the Deuteronomist author reflects the anxiety, anger, and sadness experienced as the fortunes of the Judean kingdom tumbled towards destruction and exile in the sixth century B.C.E. (see Greenberg 1972, 349). The Israelites didn't enter the land with the cry for *kherem* on their lips; rather, they left it with a pathetic hindsight, a retrospective formula for salvation, something like, "If only we had removed these pagan nations, there would have been no one to lead us to temptation, to worship their idols for which we are now being punished." Only this frustration over a failed opportunity can ex-plain the amazing proximity we find in Deuteronomy of God's love for us with the hardness we must show the dangerous Other.[20]

Comment

Clearly, texts with violence do not necessarily preach violence and violent texts do not necessarily produce violent acts or people. Certainly, they may cause us to squirm with embarrassment[21] for the fact that extremist positions (e.g., those of the Deuteronomist) became canonized, but those extremist texts don't have the force to overcome the powerful counter-tendency within the tradition towards peace, which leads us into the peace passages.

SOME STATEMENTS ON PEACE IN JUDAISM

Major rabbinic texts from late antiquity eloquently declare: "*Gadol Hashalom*"[22]—peace is the highest of values. To establish the precise direction the concept of peace will take in Judaism, it is helpful to study the context in which the word "peace" appears in the Hebrew Bible (translations from the New English Bible):[23]

I will grant peace to the land,
and you shall lie down to sleep with no one to terrorize you.

(Lev. 26: 6)

Shall not peace and truth be in my life.

(2 Kings 20:19)

Righteousness shall yield peace
and its fruit be quietness and confidence forever.

(Isa. 32:17)

Love and fidelity have come together,
justice and peace join hands.

(Ps. 85:11)

My (God's) peace is love and mercy.

(Jer. 16:5)

As Schwarzschild writes:

An adequate though informal definition of *shalom* as used in biblical, rabbinic and subsequent literatures is approximated when people say that the peace they seek is not merely the absence of war, or even of private violence, but the presence and continual growth of all creative human powers. The many variants of the etymological root of *shalom* in Hebrew usage make it clear that the basic idea can perhaps best be rendered in English by such terms as wholeness, integrity, etc.... Within that ethical totality called peace or wholeness all other human virtues and values are therefore subsumed. In such texts, to which many others could be added, truth, justice, righteousness, and grace are all collapsed into one value, and other moral values could easily be conjoined...peace is the word that designates the achievement of all human values in concert...when any significant one of them is left out not only will peace fail to be

127
.
.
.
.

achieved, but also the others may, for lack of balance, easily come into conflict with one another. (Schwarzschild 1980, 17-18)

While individuals in the Bible use the word for peace, *shalom*, to apply to their personal state of affairs, it would seem more appropriate to apply the category of *shalom* to a collective people. The following passages could be expounded to teach that the individual cannot break away from the public to seek a private peace:

> [Contrary to the surrounding] I will do my thing and peace will dwell upon me. (Deut. 29:18)

> I am peace, but when I speak, they opt for war.
>
> (Ps. 120:6-7)

> Be of the disciples of Aaron, loving peace, pursuing peace, loving one's fellow men and bringing them close to the Torah. (*Mishnah* Avot 1:12)

Thus, peace functions inclusively. The only way to ensure peace is to share it.

NONVIOLENCE IN JEWISH TEXTS

On the interpersonal level, while the Hebrew Bible doesn't explicitly demand or expect a totally nonviolent lifestyle (Leibowitz 1982, 174), it commands the love of one's neighbor and sees love as the proper response to situations of conflict that breed hatred and vengeance:

> Do not hate your brother in your heart; reprove him, and be sinless. Do not take revenge or harbor a grudge, rather love your neighbor as yourself; I am YHWH. (Lev. 19:17-18)

Relating to this passage, the medieval French exegete, Yosef Bechor Shor,[24] asks: How does God expect one who has been wronged to the point of wanting to take revenge to love one's neighbor? One thus sees the wisdom in the way Hillel of the first century paraphrased this: "That which is hateful unto you, do not do to your comrade" as the central principle of Judaic verse (Bavli Shabbat 31a). Bechor Shor finds the answer in the last, overlooked phrase of the passage: "I am YHWH: Let your love for Me overcome your hatred for him, and keep you from taking revenge; in this way love vanquishes hatred, and peace will come between you." This is the way of the Torah, "whose ways are pleasant, and all of whose paths are peace" (Prov. 3:17).

128

The Bible's desire to limit vengeance is concretized in the institution of Cities of Refuge. These places were created to protect the accidental murderer from being hunted down by avenging relatives. Capital punishment, so prevalent in the Bible's penal system, is virtually eliminated in the first major post-biblical code of Jewish law, the *Mishnah* (second century C.E.). The rabbis who compiled the *Mishnah* insisted on unrealistically severe laws of evidence in capital cases, indicating that they were not willing to allow human courts to take human life and risk irreversible miscarriages of justice. The result of their judicial caution is remarkably in line with the suggestion that among the Ten Commandments, *lo tirtzakh*, prohibits manslaughter as well as murder.

It is instructive to examine an illustrative case of rabbinic discussion in order to see how the scriptural, and then rabbinic, tradition is taken up and made a part of the ongoing life of the Jewish faith. For example, the popular notion that Judaism commands the preemptive killing of an attacker intent on homicide ("*haba l'horgecha, hashkem l'horgo*") disregards the fact that, far from being dogmatic or prescriptive, the quotation under discussion is but a midrashic resolution of an unintelligible verse from a biblical narrative. In the biblical narrative, David does *not* kill Saul, even though Saul has made his lethal intentions known for some time and acted upon them (1 Sam. 24:9). The Masoretic reading, "*v'amar l'harogcha vatakhos alecha*," seems corrupt, and the rabbis determine that David is referring to a teaching from *torah shebehalpeh* ("*v'amra Torah ...*") that would have justified his killing Saul. This quote is borrowed from its original context (Talmud Bavli Brachot 62b) and then applied ("*l'halacha*") in case law for justifiable homicide, in the extreme case of the thief intruding into a home in the dark (Talmud Bavli, Sanhedrin 72a-b, on Ex. 22:1).

The rabbis explain the Torah's exempting of the killer from punishment by constructing the following chain of cause and effect: The thief has assumed that the homeowner is prepared to attack him and is therefore willing, in self-defense, to strike the homeowner preemptively. This, in turn, justifies the homeowner's anticipatory strike (probably with a household implement, and not a weapon). The biblical passage stipulates that the homicide is not justified "if the sun has risen upon him"; one can assume that this is because

129

the homeowner can now see he is not in mortal danger and has no longer a need for a preemptive strike. However one develops the implications of this passage for the rare personal encounter, the tragic spiral of fear described here is, in my opinion, too narrow a ledge for justifying the stockpiling of lethal weapons by individuals, and certainly is not applicable to situations of international conflict.

REJECTION OF MILITARISM

Judaism's long-standing rejection of militarism predominates in Jewish texts of every age. The Book of Deuteronomy warns Israel against taking pride in its military successes and imagining them to be independently achieved; it sees these attitudes as the height of human pride and folly and dangerously close to idolatry:

> Take care lest you forget YHWH your God…lest you eat well, build good houses and dwell in them, prosper…and say to yourself: it is through my might and prowess that I have all this. (Deut. 8:11-18)

In fact, it would be a mistake for Israel to imagine that it was morally virtuous enough to merit its material inheritance; it is rather that others were worse than they, and also that God needed to fulfill the promise made to the Patriarchs (Deut. 9:5).

This anti-militarist attitude is reflected in the downplaying of the role of the Hasmoneans in the Tana'itic explanations of the origins of Hanukkah. The prophetic reading (*haftarah*) chosen by the rabbis for the Sabbath that falls during Hanukkah includes the famous verse from Zachariah: Not by force or by might, but with My spirit, says the Lord (Deut. 4:6), which is at the core of the nineteenth-century universalist, pre-Zionist understanding of Hanukkah.[25] Similarly, we find statements against Bar Kochva whose unsuccessful revolt against the Romans in 132-135 C.E. brought even more devastation to the Jews of Palestine than the Great Revolt of 70 C.E., in which the Second Temple and Jerusalem were destroyed.[26] Until recent years, the military profession was so antithetical to the heart and experience of the Jew that the Passover Haggadah found in a Jewish home was likely to portray the wicked son as a soldier. (By contrast, a Haggadah published by the Israeli Ministry of Defense Publishing House, *circa* 1970, shows glossy pictures of the devastation of the Egyptian army in Sinai during the 1967 war as a modern update of the 10 plagues of antiquity.)

ISAIAH 2 AS THE IDEAL

One can hardly begin to outline the expressions of the ideal of peace, and the age of peace, any better than by citing the book named for the late eighth-century Prophet, Isaiah of Jerusalem, which reads:

> At the end of days, the mount of the house of YHWH will be established at the top of the mountains, raised above hills, and all peoples will stream to it. Many nations will begin to say, "Let us go up to the mount of YHWH, to the house of the God of Jacob, so that he teach us his ways, and we will follow his paths, for teaching will go out of Zion, YHWH's word from Jerusalem. He will adjudicate among the peoples, and discipline many nations; they will break down their swords into shovels, their spears into pruning hooks: nations will not raise swords against each other, not train for war any more. (Isa. 2:2-4)

More important, however, are the texts that indicate a clear perception of the importance of such sentiments in Jewish life. Notable in the following series of comments are the teachings of R. Yohanan Ben Zakkai, who was famous for enlisting Roman support for the establishment of the rabbinic seat at Yavne and thereby exercising a nonviolent alternative to the disastrous Great Revolt initiated by Jewish zealots (whose suppression led to the destruction of the Second Temple and the destruction of Jerusalem):

> One is not allowed to carry neither a sword nor a bow, nor a shield nor a club nor a spear [on the Sabbath], and if one is carried, an expiatory sacrifice must be brought. Rabbi Eliezer says, [it is allowed because] they are considered as ornament. The sages respond, [they cannot be considered as ornaments because] they are loathsome, as it is written, "They shall grind their swords into plowshares, and their spears into pruning hooks; nation shall not lift up sword against nation, neither shall they learn war any more (Isa. 2:4)." (*Mishnah* Shabbat 6:4)

In Exodus, we find the admonition: "If you build an altar to me (God) do not use hewn stones, for your sword will have been raised on it, thereby defiling it" (Ex. 20:22). In this connection, Rabbi Simon ben Eleazar used to say, "The altar is made to prolong the years of man and iron is made to shorten the years of man; it is not right for that which shortens life to be lifted up against that which prolongs life."

Rabbi Yohanan ben Zakkai says of this passage from Deuteronomy,

> Behold it says, 'Thou shall build...of whole stones.' They are to be
> stones that establish peace. Now, by using the method of *kal
> vakhomer*, you reason: If, in the case of the stones for the altar, which
> do not see nor hear nor speak, yet, because they serve to establish
> peace between Israel and their Father in heaven, the Holy One,
> blessed be He: 'Thou shalt lift no iron tool upon them, how much
> more so should he who establishes peace between human beings,
> between husband and wife, between city and city, between nation
> and nation, between family and family, between government and
> government be protected so that no harm come to him.' (Deut. 27:6)

How does one draw practical guidance from such reflection? Note
that justice and peace, according to Isaiah 2, are integrally connected. The order of these two elements is critical: first, justice is
established, and only afterwards does peace become a reality. The
aggrieved party is not expected to give up his claim and be pacified;
on the contrary, he has the right and the obligation to demand
justice. Peace without justice is surrender, which, when achieved
under the guise of peace, is built on the flimsy foundations of false-
hood; it only plants the seeds of future oppression. Attempts at
reconciliation initiated before injustice is redressed can theoreti-
cally still lead to nonviolent conflict resolution, but they force the
disadvantaged party to rely on the goodwill of the oppressor to
yield not to pressure but rather through persuasion—an assumption which goes against the very experience of oppression.

OF ISAIAH'S VISION OF JERUSALEM—THEN AND NOW

For contemporary Judaism, the question is inevitably asked: In
what way can this passage be applied to the Israeli-Palestinian conflict? The following rabbinic statement is found in the *Mishnah*
(third century C.E./A.D.): The world is based on three elements:
justice, truth, and peace (Avot 1). This is a paraphrase of Isaiah's
doctrine. The statement is important for us because it transfers the
realm of responsibility from the eschatological and the divine to
the present and the human. Justice, truth, and peace are interconnected and mutually dependent; they must be aspired to, and can
be approached, if not attained, through the ongoing human commitment to and search for God's word.

Justice is a simple concept that is well understood instinctively. It is the assurance of equitable treatment. In situations of dispute, attaining justice depends on distilling the truth in front of an objective judge who has the confidence of both parties and whose judgment results in the restoration of peace. However, what works for individuals or groups within a society with an implied or explicit social contract may be hard to apply internationally. It is very hard for different countries to agree on and give authority to an outside power. Thus, the absence of a judge who is perceived to have the inherent right to judge is a major impediment to the resolution of international conflict. Secondly, established governments tend not to recognize the legitimacy of "popular committees" or other un-incorporated nongovernmental organizations. The very notion of the equality of the disputants cannot be taken for granted. And finally, the idea of the natural rights of a nation, which correspond to that of individuals, must be investigated.

While it may be relatively simple for individuals or communities to establish, through religious principles or on humanist grounds, the inviolability of life, liberty, and the pursuit of happiness for individual human beings, it will be harder to do so for nations; there may not be a basis for evaluating competing myths of nationhood or for establishing group rights to which other groups must yield. But giving up on the establishment of international justice means acknowledging that the world is a jungle where only the fittest survive.

The most tragic abdication of religion and reason by Zionists regarding their obligation towards justice in the Israeli-Palestinian conflict is in the general legitimization given to the usurpation of the land of the Palestinian refugees. Palestinians' claim to their ancestral land is not political or geo-political, as is the right of national self-determination, which can only be realized within the limitations of political structures. The right of individuals to their homes is primary and undeniable and no amount of apologetics or global shuffling can eradicate it. The demand for the restitution of the refugees to their land is seen by virtually all Israeli Jews as tantamount to the dismantling of the state of Israel and the disintegration of Israeli Jewish society. Yet, the lack of progress towards the resolution of this issue not only dooms Israelis and Palestinians to perpetual violent struggle but it also negates the basis of, and perhaps even de-legitimizes, the very existence of the state of Israel.

A JEWISH GIFT

Judaism has a tool that must be activated for this situation: *takanat hashavim*, the ordinance for a compassionate justice in the restoration of misappropriated property: In the past, in order to encourage a thief to return stolen property, the strict rules of restoration required one who had misappropriated a wooden beam (and already used it to build a roof) to dismantle whatever the stolen beam had been used for and to restore the very same beam. In later times, rabbis have allowed for the beam's value to be paid. In our case, we could use this principle to foster a gradual restoration of Arab homes—built by Palestinians before 1948 and involuntarily surrendered when the refugees were expelled or fled in fear—to the descendants of the original owners. Jewish homes or neighborhoods built on expropriated or "abandoned" Palestinian land could be maintained so long as equivalent plots of land be given to the heirs instead. Thus, *takanat hashavim*, applied assiduously but compassionately, would work towards the restoration of Palestinian roots without visiting trauma on Jews. Jews could thus be brought to recognize the higher good involved in their making room for the fulfillment of the dreams of other "lovers of Zion."

Isaiah's vision posits the involvement of YHWH as adjudicator in national disputes and the willingness of the nations to accept YHWH's decision as a result of the universal acceptance of YHWH as God. In the context of modern international, interreligious conflict resolution, there clearly has to be found an agency of similar authority. In the absence of unanimously accepted, supernatural revelation, the best we can aspire to is a pooling of the collective wisdom of humanity—a synthesis of the divine as revealed to all societies throughout history. The practical translation of this vision is an inspired United Nations dedicated to human and environmental survival through the agency of the constituent member nations.

134

The reciprocal relationship between inner peace and interpersonal peace requires us, as it does all religious leaders, to recognize the religious imperative to contribute to peacemaking. This involves strengthening trust between individuals and congregations through fostering dialogue and positive human encounters. This, in turn, will foster the understanding that establishing the truth is a dialogical and dialectical process:[27] One side and one text cannot possibly contain all the truth but each human encounter can move us closer to the truth. We are dependent on each other for arriving at the truth which our sources contain. We are, in fact, each other's most indispensable resource.

BIBLIOGRAPHY

Bleich, J. David. *Contemporary Halakhic Problems*. Vol. 1. New York: Ktav Publishing House and Yeshiva University Press, 1977.

Friedman, Maurice. "Hasidism and the Love of Enemies." In *The Challenge of Shalom: The Jewish Tradition of Peace and Justice*, ed. Murray Polner and Naomi Goodman, 40-48. Philadelphia: New Society Publishers, 1994.

Greenberg, Moshe. "Herem." In *Encyclopedia Judaica*, vol. 8, 344-350. Jerusalem: Keter Publishing House, 1972.

Harkabi, Yehoshafat. *The Bar Kokhba Syndrome: Risk and Realism in International Politics*. Chappaqua: Rossel Books, 1983.

Leibowitz, Yeshayahu. "War and Heroism in Israel, Past and Present." In *Faith, History and Values* (Hebrew). Jerusalem: Akademon Press, 1982.

Muffs, Yochanan. *Love and Joy: Law, Language and Religion in Ancient Israel*. New York: The Jewish Theological Seminary of America, 1992.

Polner, Murray and Naomi Goodman, ed. *The Challenge of Shalom: The Jewish Tradition of Peace and Justice*. Philadelphia: New Society Publishers, 1994.

Schwartz, Richard. *Judaism and Global Survival*. New York: Vantage, 1984.

Schwarzschild, Steven S. "*Shalom*." In *The Challenge of Shalom: The Jewish Tradition of Peace and Justice*, ed. Murray Polner and Naomi Goodman, 16-25. Philadelphia: New Society Publishers, 1994.

Wald, M. *Jewish Teaching on Peace*. New York: Bloch, 1944.

Yuval, Yisrael. "Vengeance and Damnation, Blood and Defamation: From Jewish Martyrdom to Blood Libel Accusations." In *Zion*, vol. 58, no. 1 (1993).

NOTES

[1] A literal translation from the Hebrew, which is highly irregular. This leaves it up to the reader/worshipper to decide whether the author is actually saying "I am peace," or perhaps "I am at peace," "I am with peace," or "I am for peace."

[2] With the roots of Israel's intellectual and political elite being basically Marxist, it may not be surprising for its culture to have Bolshevik characteristics.

[3] "Happy are you, people of Israel, peerless, redeemed by God, your protecting shield, *for whom the sword is your pride* [or *who is the sword of your pride*]." The syntax is ambiguous: does the phrase modify God, like the phrase before it, or is it

elliptic, modifying Israel? In Deuteronomy, which constantly attributes all of Israel's military successes to God (Deut. 8:11-18), the latter is more likely. Medieval Jewish commentators Saadia Gaon and Sforno favored this interpretation.

[4] The singular is popularly thought to take a variant form, *talmid khacham*, meaning either "a student of a sage," which suggests that wisdom and authority can be derived from a single personality, or "a wise student," which gives the student a higher standing than allowed by tradition. I thank Professor Shmuel Safrai of Hebrew University for this information.

[5] An ironic, yet indicative, result of this supreme emphasis on *torah shebbehalpeh* is that in a yeshivah high school "secular subjects" include Bible classes.

[6] Including those surrounding Jesus (the Jew) of Nazareth.

[7] David J. Bleich, *Contemporary Halakhic Problems*, vol. 1 (New York: Ktav Publishing House and Yeshiva University Press, 1977), 244-269. Bleich points out that so many technical issues remain unclear that one cannot speak of a halachic preparedness for a non-supernatural reinstitution of the sacrificial cult.

[8] See the arguments and imagery of the eulogy, *"Baruch Hagever,"* written in memory of IDF Captain Baruch Goldstein, M.D., who massacred 29 worshipping Muslims in the Ibrahimiye Mosque/Cave of Machpelah on Purim, 1994.

[9] Calling this reading "Torah" is not a public relations ploy designed to achieve the imprimatur of tradition. Instead, it expresses the conviction that God's living word is true to the extent that it allows for a multiplicity of interpretations. Recent interpretations emerging seem to contradict or to surpass earlier understandings.

[10] This passage surely resonates in the famous response of Jesus to Peter, that he must forgive seventy times seven (Matt. 18:22).

[11] In this passage, Rabbi Meir prays for the death of troublesome highwaymen and Bruria responds with: "Is such a prayer permitted? It is written: 'Let sins cease,' not sinners. Further, look at the end of the verse: 'And let wicked people be no more.' Since sins will cease, there will be no more wicked people. Rather, pray that they should repent."

[12] See Maurice Friedman, "Hasidism and the Love of Enemies," in *The Challenge of Shalom: The Jewish Tradition of Peace and Justice"* (Philadelphia: New Society Publishers, 1964), 45-46.

[13] We don't hear of casualties in this and many other battle descriptions in the Bible. The Israelites actually report that all their men survived the victorious war against the Midianites (Nm. 31:49), which in today's Israeli newspeak would be formulated as "all our forces returned *b'shalom.*"

[14] On the relatively rare occasions that the Patriarchs invoke God in their relationships with others, it is not to claim privilege but rather to indicate a state of blessedness and to justify their own self-denial and generosity (14:22-24; 33:10-11; 39:9; 41:51-52; 42:18; 43:29; but cf. 45:9 when Joseph almost regresses to power-hungriness). The model of their reliance on God is Genesis 15:6, "And because he [Abraham] put his trust in the Lord, He reckoned it to his merit" (new JPS translation).

[15] Compared to chapters 1-11 of Genesis, and the rest of the Torah, in this part of the book of Genesis, God maintains a private presence. God is active in fulfilling the promise of continuity, intervening to protect the wives (Sara 12:17 and

20:3-7, 17-18; Hagar, 16 and 21) and relatives (Lot and his family, 18-19); helping the Patriarchs find wives (24, and implicitly, by giving Jacob extraordinary strength, in 29) and solving infertility and difficult pregnancies (18, 21, 25, and 30), and by bringing Joseph to Egypt, masterminding the survival of the family, and through them, a multitude of people (45:5; 50:20). It seems as if the god we need for our families and for global survival is a much more gentle god than the one that our national existence requires.

[16] This is one of many insights I gained from Yisrael Knol's seminar on Jewish Theology given at the *Shalom* Hartman Institute, 1995.

[17] The wars again Sihon and Og, in the Transjordan, are reported twice: in Nm. 21, a complete military victory is recorded; in Deut. 2:31-3:7, the institution of an almost total *kherem*—the cattle are spared and taken as booty—is added. Perhaps the Deuteronomist regards the Transjordan as a part of the Promised Land.

[18] Similarly, Pinchas is awarded a "covenant of peace" right after driving his spear through the Israelite and Moabite idolaters (Nm. 25:1-15).

[19] See Yerushalmi Shevi'it 6:1, in which Joshua is seen to have followed the more flexible laws of Deut. 20:10-15 in apparently disregarding verses 16-18.

[20] One frequently sees a rapid shift in the emotions of the Deuteronomist author wherever the stakes are high or highly charged memories are recalled; for instance, in Deut. 23:4-7, in the passage forbidding the absorption of the Amonite or Moabite into the Israelite people, we find a relatively long description of their inhospitability in the desert and Moab's attempt to have Israel cursed by Balaam. This description flows into a theocentric description of Israel's release from that predicament and then into a sudden transition from the recalling of God's love for Israel to a ferocious commandment to maintain eternal hostility towards them.

[21] For those who venerate the text, this apprehension is much worse than embarrassment; it is *khilul hashem*, desecration of God's name, and brings with it deep soul-searching and acts of penitence. Thus, the raising of consciousness of the problematic nature of text is the first step toward energizing a religious peace camp.

[22] *Gadol Hashalom*—"Great is Peace," a phrase that appears in a number of places in rabbinic literature, is best known as the refrain in an extensive section in *Midrash Raba* (and parallel collections) on the Priestly Blessing, Nm. 6:22-27, which ends with "may God grant you peace." While the rhetorical intention of *gadol* ("great") is actually the superlative ("the *greatest* [value] is peace"), one must remember that the rabbis make ultimate claims for the supremacy of various commandments (e.g., observing the Sabbath and studying the Torah).

[23] For a fuller collection of scriptural quotations on peace, see Wald 1944; Schwartz 1984 cites additional anthologies of classical Jewish statements on peace.

[24] This relatively obscure source was brought to the attention of the students of his Schechter Institute rabbinical School seminar by Professor Moshe Greenberg.

[25] Compare the original medieval text of "Maoz Tzur" to the nineteenth-century adaptation by Leopold Stein, rendered in English by Jastrow and Gottheil and known as "Rock of Ages." We bring here the first and last verses of the origi-

nal, skipping the four middle historical verses retelling the stories of Exodus, Exile, and Restoration, the downfall of Haman, and the victory of the Maccabees:

> Fortress, rock of my salvation
> It is proper to praise you
> My temple will be established
> And there we will offer a thanksgiving offering
> When You prepare a slaughter
> Of the blaspheming enemy
> I will complete the dedication of the altar
> With the singing of a psalm
>
> Expose your holy arm
> And hasten the end, salvation
> Avenge the blood of your servants
> From the wicked nation
> The hour is late
> There is no end to the bad days
> Reject the red one,
> In the shadow of Zalmon
> Raise up seven shepherds

The nineteenth-century version reads:

> Rock of Ages let our song
> Praise Thy saving power;
> Thou amidst the raging foes
> Wast our shelt'ring tower.
> Furious they assailed us
> But Thine arm availed us
> And Thy word
> Broke Their sword
> When our own strength failed us
>
> Kindling new the holy lamps
> Priests approved in suffering
> Purified the nation's shrine
> Brought to God their offering.
> And His courts surrounding
> Hear in joy abounding
> Happy throngs
> Singing songs
> With a mighty sounding.
>
> Children of the martyr race
> Whether free or fettered
> Wake the echoes of the songs
> Where ye may be scattered.
> Yours the message cheering
> That the time is nearing
> Which will see
> All men free
> Tyrants disappearing.

The original calls for apocalyptic violence and revenge ending in an eschatological restoration of sacrificial ritual in the only place it is allowed, the Temple Mount. This original version is particularistic and resonates with anti-Christian polemic. The nineteenth-century version, by contrast, is inclusive ("all men free") and universally non-territorial ("where ye may be scattered"), relegating the priestly ritual to the past (middle verse). It, too, is eschatologically pulsating but redefines the Jewish mission as the fight against tyranny.

[26] For recent thoughts along these same lines by a modern Israeli military leader, cf. Harkabi 1983.

[27] See the works of Martin Buber. Cf. the prayer for peace by Rabbi Nahman of Bratzlav (nineteenth century): "There should be no hatred, jealousy, rivalry, triumphalism or pettiness between people, only love and a great peace, that everyone should experience love from one another, and be sure that each wants good to befall the other, and to love them and for them to succeed, so that all could come together and speak with each other and explain the truth to one another."

Chapter 8

POLITICAL ATHEISM AND RADICAL FAITH: THE CHALLENGE OF CHRISTIAN NONVIOLENCE IN THE THIRD MILLENNIUM

By Daniel L. Smith-Christopher

You have heard that it was said, 'You shall love your neighbor and hate your enemy.' But I say to you, Love your enemies and pray for those who persecute you.

Jesus of Nazareth, Matthew

Live in harmony with one another; do not be haughty, but associate with the lowly; do not claim to be wiser than you are. Do not repay anyone evil for evil, but take thought for what is noble in the sight of all. If it is possible, so far as it depends on you, live peaceably with all.

Paul of Tarsus, Romans

Do not be astonished, brothers and sisters, that the world hates you.

1 John

This essay is a reflection on the apparently strange juxtaposition of the three New Testament passages listed above. How could the seeking of peace result in the hatred and the animosity of wider society? The answer, I would argue, cuts to the heart of the modern issue of Christian nonviolence in the late twentieth century and may well force Christians to face the full implication of what non-

DR. DANIEL L. SMITH-CHRISTOPHER is associate professor of theological studies and director of the Peace Studies Program at Loyola Marymount University in Los Angeles. Dr. Smith-Christopher, a life-long member of the Society of Friends (Quakers), has published numerous articles in both Biblical Studies and Peace Studies and is the author of *The Religion of the Landless* (1989) and the "Commentary on Daniel" for *The New Interpreter's Bible* (1997), and is among the authors of the upcoming *Oxford Bible Commentary*. Dr. Smith-Christopher has also edited a collection on cultural interpretation of the Bible: *Text and Experience: Toward a Cultural Exegesis of the Bible* (1995). Before beginning his teaching, Daniel Smith-Christopher served as a volunteer Quaker peace research worker in Israel/Palestine between 1985-1987.

violence actually means as a religious value—namely, a direct challenge to the concept of nationalism.

The title of this essay is taken from an aspect of early Christian relations with Roman imperial society in the first three hundred years of Christianity. Because the early Christians refused to honor or participate in the state religion, Christians were frequently, and ironically, accused of "atheism." They did not "believe in" (as we would say today) the national gods of Rome. They certainly refused to deify and worship the emperor. This act of political defiance is what I refer to as "political atheism." I believe it is an appropriately provocative way to speak of radical Christian commitment to nonviolence.

The important partner with political atheism is "radical faith"— a Christian radical faithfulness to Jesus that interrogates and challenges all forms of nationalism, patriotism, and cults of violence that are so much a part of modern warfare and its preparations. Retired Professor Colonel Harry G. Summers has written that "the passions of the people...are the engines of war." If this is so, then Christian nonviolence, which is a radical faith, must renew the call to political atheism in the twenty-first century just as it called Christians to political atheism in the first centuries of the Christian movement.

The dominant Christian position in relation to warfare is the doctrine of the "just war. Although it does not have the status of official doctrine in the Roman Catholic Church, just war is certainly the predominant tradition. In some mainstream Protestant traditions, the just war doctrine most certainly does have confessional status. I contend that radical Christian commitment to nonviolence at the end of the twentieth century does not, in fact, struggle against a calm or reasoned proposition of the just war doctrine. In the modern world, to apply the just war doctrine simply requires too much information for Christians to be able to determine if a particular war is just or not. Tom Engelhardt, in his recent analysis of the culture of war (he refers to it as "The Culture of Victory") in the United States, suggests that already in the 1950s:

> the world could be fathomed only by adepts...Electronic "eyes" and "ears" picked up the enemy worldwide, but their products could be interpreted only by "cryptanalysts, traffic analysts, photographic in-

terpreters, and telemetry, radar, and signal analysts…who produced material for, at best, a few thousand people with high enough security clearances to see the finished intelligence product.… Least equipped for the new struggle was the public. (Engelhardt 1995, 116)

In such circumstances where we have little available, reliable information, how are we to go about ethical decision-making? Does not the just war doctrine become, in the absence of real information in the era of hyper-managed media coverage, merely a form of rallying the masses rather than encouraging true debate? When so much information is "top secret," we are asked merely to "have faith" in our leaders. The religious connotation is suggestive. Christian nonviolence confronts this virtual *religious zeal* for violence expressed in notions like: "father/mother-land," "national home-land," or expressed in carefully (and often literally) orchestrated calls to "stand to the last man," "defend our way of life," "never back down." In short, modern warfare is fueled more by emotionalism and patriotic jingoism than careful ethical consideration. Modern Christians radically committed to the nonviolence of Jesus face the mentality of the crusade (see Yoder 1984).

WARFARE AS RELIGION

War, as the ancients knew at least as well as the U.S. State Department, is a religion whose gods are demanding. The most successful of the empires of the ancient Near East and later, in the West, were scrupulous in their certainty that their gods of war were well-pleased, well-fed, and well-known. The unprecedented age of peace during the reign of Augustus (31 B.C.E.— 14 C.E.) was commemorated in Rome with an altar to peace, *built on the field of Mars, the god of war* (Wengst 1987, 7-19). We are beginning to understand the widespread significance of the ancient Roman emperor cult as the essential amalgam of religion, power, and the state:

> The spirit of empire ran deep and wide. The remarkable cohesion of Roman society itself at the center of the empire can only be explained by the way in which the revival of Roman religion and traditional morality was substituted for what were previously political processes…in a reconfiguration of Roman power relations…Thus, as Greeks went about their lives, they were constantly reminded of the importance of the emperor, whose presence pervaded public space. (Horsley 1997, 13, 21)

Roman society was threatened by the stubborn opposition from early Christians whose bold rejection of such activities as the emperor cult and its violence earned them the accusation of atheism. Their refusal to honor the state gods, which were of the essence of Roman identity, brought active persecution as well (Womersley 1988, 99-133; Vogt 1965, 82-83). Religion and power are always a tempting mix. Yet, centuries later, it is still true that if one challenges the gods of war—whether they are national, ethnic, or religious—in the name of Christianity, this is tantamount to standing against the tide of Western civilization and its *own* gods.

In short, to assert a faith that embraces the nonviolence of Jesus is to proclaim oneself an atheist in relation to the preferred gods of nationalism and patriotism. This assertion of faith becomes all the more difficult when such war jingoism incorporates the language of the Bible and Christian faith. Thus, the challenge of modern nonviolence in the Christian tradition is to proclaim radical faith *and* political atheism, a proclamation that has repercussions for both the Church and the state.

ROME OR THE KINGDOM OF GOD: "YOU CANNOT SERVE GOD AND MAMMON"

Recently, there has been some debate about the nonviolence of the earliest Christians, with some scholars suggesting that Christians refused Roman military service because of its religious requirements as much as, or perhaps more than, any aversion to killing (see Hunter 1992). In fact, many of the early Christian martyrs who refused military service did so precisely because participation in military service amounted to participation in a rival religion—a religion which mandated violent activities. Marcellus, circa 298 C.E., was martyred soon after proclaiming his clear perception of the connection of violence with nationalist religious zeal:

> I am a soldier of Jesus Christ, the eternal king. From now I cease to serve your emperors and I despise the worship of your gods of wood and stone.... It is not fitting that a Christian, who fights for Christ his Lord, should be a soldier according to the brutalities of this world. (Hornus 1960, 133-135)

Such witnesses are not unusual in the early centuries of Christianity. By the fourth and fifth centuries C.E. nonviolence in Christianity had come to be considered both a minority position and a heresy. To this day, it remains in an adversarial position to the majority of traditions in Christianity. Indeed, although there are many divisive issues of practice and belief which modern Christians have decided are no longer worthy of acrimonious debate, there is yet no peace on the issue of peace. This is due, in no small measure, to the fact that few issues other than the debate on war and its widespread "Christian" support reveal Christians in a more shameful display of self-interested sophistry—a tradition dating at least to Augustine and perpetuated by Aquinas (see Marrin 1971, 52-73).

Christian nonviolence is the refusal to be moved by flag and state. It is also the refusal to participate in the liturgies of destruction and in the hymnic glorification of violence as national epic and identity (see Engelhardt 1995). In short, Christian nonviolence is political atheism in the name of radical faith in Jesus, who commands his followers to love even the enemy. Indeed, as Klassen points out, the love of enemies is the strongest assertion by Jesus. Christian compassion is to know no national or ethnic or political boundaries (Klassen 1984, 84-92). Jesus was aware that his message would divide old loyalties and create new ones. Jesus said that his word would be like a "sword" that would divide even family loyalties. The passage concludes with Jesus' teaching that "one's foes will be members of one's own household" (Matt. 10:34-36). This is an image borrowed from the "verbal swords" of the Hebrew Prophets (Isa. 49:2; Jer. 25:16; cf. Job 5:15). Such expectations of new social formulations match precisely the call to love enemies.

JESUS AS NONVIOLENT RABBI

It is often argued, even by those who advocate the nonviolence of Jesus, that nonviolence was a new teaching. But the Gospel teachings of Jesus of Nazareth with respect to violence are consistent with other Hebrew/Jewish developments, such as quietism and a nonviolent ethos among the early teachers of Pharasaic Judaism (see Kimmelman 1968; Genot-Bismuth 1981). Nonviolence is most certainly reflected in the teachings of R. Yochanon Ben Zakkai—nearly a contemporary of Jesus—whose peaceful teachings included his rejection of the ill-fated war against Rome in 67-70 C.E.; his own bias in favor of the widely noted Pharasaic loathing of capital punishment; his favorable comments on military exemptions in Deuteronomy 20; and his famous meditation on peacemakers as "stones of God's altar." Peacemakers are, metaphorically, like the literal stones used to build altars (Deut. 27:6). Peacemakers should have no contact with iron (and by implication, then, with weapons) (Neusner 1962; Neusner 1970; in this volume, Milgrom).

Notably, however, the pacifist teachings of Jesus are nowhere explicit in the context of making ethical decisions with regard to participating in warfare *per se*. The question, "Shall we fight in the military?" was a non-question for Jews of Palestine, a territory occupied by Rome. The question for a Jew of first-century Palestine with respect to lethal violence was a question about the tactics of resistance to the occupying powers. In virtually all cases, Jesus' teachings about "loving enemies" and "praying for those who persecute you" applied to relations with the occupying power. Marcus Borg, arguably one of the most important contemporary scholars of the historical Jesus, has written:

> Jesus said, in deliberate contrast to the limitation of love to one's compatriot, 'Love your enemies'.... What would this have meant in teachings directed to Israel in the late twenties of the first century? It had an inescapable and identifiable political implication: the non-Jewish enemy was, above all, Rome. To say 'Love your enemies' would have meant, "Love the Romans; do not join the resistance movement," whatever other implications it might have had. (Borg 1998, 136-146)

In short, Jesus' teaching was intended to overturn the so-called patriotism that would call for killing the enemy. The most significant location of Jesus' ethical teachings in relation to violence is in the body of teachings that the Gospel of Matthew calls, "The Sermon on the Mount." There, beginning already in one of the famous blessings, Jesus honors peacemakers:

> Blessed are the peacemakers, for they will be called the children of God. (Matt. 5:9)

Later in the discourse, Jesus elaborates on this peacemaking, and especially how his teaching differs from the expected traditions of behavior:

You have heard it said, 'An eye for an eye and a tooth for a tooth'. But I say to you, Do not resist an evildoer. But if anyone strikes you on the right cheek, turn the other also.... You have heard it said 'You shall love your neighbor and hate your enemy.' But I say to you, Love your enemies and pray for those who persecute you. (Matt. 5:38-48)

Even when a disciple took up a sword to defend Jesus himself, Jesus commanded that he put the sword away, for: "all who take up the sword will perish by the sword" (Matt. 26:52).

What is certainly clear is that Jesus' teaching on violence was understood by early Christians as speaking directly to the issue of participation in lethal violence, even in the cause of national defense. For the first three centuries of Christianity, the normative interpretation of the teachings of Jesus by Christians was that obedience to Christ precluded participation in the military. But more must be said. What is clear in the teachings of Jesus is how his advocacy of peacefulness is tied to his view of the nature of the community he founded. Christian nonviolence was not a general ethical maxim. It was a rule for the community of disciples and followers, directing them in the way they were to live in the midst of those who lived quite differently:

Jesus called to them and said, 'You know that among the Gentiles those whom they recognize as their rulers lord it over them, and their great ones are tyrants over them. But it is not so among you, but whoever wishes to become great among you must be your servant.' (Mark 10:42-43)

Although there is nothing in the Gospel portraits of Jesus that contradicts the pacifism of Jesus, there are occasionally noted objections (see Yoder 1994; Anderson 1994). One such classic objection is the phrase, "Think not that I come to bring peace, I have come to bring a sword." But this phrase, as has already been noted, appears in the context of how Christian faith may divide former loyalties—even within the family. Jesus resolves this apparent contradiction with a teaching totally consistent with loving enemies: "one's foes become a part of one's household" (Matt 10:36).

The famous cleansing of the Temple episode, where Jesus overturns the tables of the moneylenders (noted in all four Gospels), is often cited as inconsistent with a peace-loving Jesus. None of the accounts of this episode implied that Jesus actually engaged in bodily harm to those gathered in the Temple complex. But such action as Jesus exhibited is just as readily an illustration for the form of non-violence that Jesus does advocate—active, resistant, and interested in public, prophetic demonstration. This is in the tradition of prophets like Jeremiah and Isaiah (both of whom are explicitly invoked by Jesus in his famed "house of prayer/den of robbers" image drawn from Jeremiah 7:11 and Isaiah 56:7). In short, the Temple episode is only inconsistent with a weak passivism—one that is too often set up by Christian advocates of a nonviolent Jesus (see Hiller 1966, 27-49).

The "Old Testament": Toward a Hebraic Nonviolence

On a widespread popular level, what Christians refer to as the "Old Testament" is often *functionally* ignored in Christian faith and practice. Yet, there have always been voices within the Christian tradition that call for a serious Christian theology of the Old Testament (Ollenburger 1992, 1991; Brueggemann 1997). However, for the vast majority of contemporary Christians, in both Catholic and Protestant traditions, the Old Testament remains largely a source of Sunday School stories for children. It is also the source for the occasional conservative diatribe against sins apparently thought to be insufficiently condemned in the New Testament (such as homosexuality) and a source for the occasional prophecy about Jesus. In such contexts, the Hebrew Bible is used to defend nationalist patriotism and military bravado when it serves the purposes of Christians. It is discarded as if it doesn't apply to "us Christians" when it is not useful—for example, when attempting to blunt the nonviolence of Jesus.

When we focus on the issue of violence in the Hebrew Scriptures, we find an emphasis on the fate of the ancient Israelite state—on the conquest of the land of Canaan by the Hebrews (Josh.) and the wars of conquest engaged in by the Kings of Israel and Judah (Judg.; 2 Kings). But this is not the whole of Hebrew history. The Hebrew Bible also deals with the concept of a violent *God,* a concept apparently opposed to the perception of the peaceful Jesus of the New Testament.

Scholars deal with the contradictory portrayals of God in the two Testaments in the following ways: (a) they minimize the relationship between the Testaments by relegating the Hebrew Bible to mere background; or (b) they argue for a kind of progressive understanding of the nature of God from primitive to sophisticated (they imply that violence is primitive and peacefulness is sophisticated); or (c) they maintain that certain practices pertain to certain ages. Options (a) and (b) minimize the Jewish identity of Jesus and remove the teachings of Jesus from their continuity with the Prophetic tradition of social justice, the Wisdom traditions, and the Apocalyptic traditions; and run serious risks of fueling anti-Semitism. Furthermore, apart from the Gospels, major sections of the New Testament become unintelligible when cut off from their roots in the Hebrew tradition. Option (c), a *that was then, this is now* theology, seems a hopelessly circular argument that requires a set of criteria from outside the tradition.

LISTENING TO DEFEATS AS WELL AS VICTORIES

An alternative approach to explaining away the troubling parts of the Hebrew Bible would begin by insisting that we not only listen to the victories of war (Joshua, David, etc.) but also the defeats, and especially the defeat and exile of both Jewish states. In the context of defeat, the biblical historians pass judgment on the earlier military bravado and condemn virtually every King of Israel and Judah, with the sole exception of Josiah who is not praised for warfare but rather religious reform. It is important to note that the Hebrew Scriptures were at least edited, if not all written, *after* the failure of the monarchy. Given Israel's history of state formation and monarchy, it would have been surprising if ancient Israel did *not* provide the examples it does of lyrical self-glorious celebration of violence and power. Such bravado in the ancient Near East reaches barbaric, even grisly proportions, for example, in Neo-Assyrian inscriptions. These inscriptions arguably reached the pinnacle of excess for using sheer military terror in both practice and propaganda in ancient Near Eastern civilization. A Neo-Assyrian document records an official's response to a local village revolt as follows:

> I built a pillar over against the city-gate and I flayed all the chief men who revolted, and I covered the pillar with their skins. (noted in Saggs 1963)

149
.
.
.
.

It is also important to note that ancient warfare was always and everywhere a religious act. In their inscriptions and monuments, the Neo-Assyrians, the Egyptians, the Babylonians, the Persians, and the Greeks all maintain that war was often won by the participation not only of their own gods, but also that of the gods of their defeated enemies (Cogan 1974, 6; cf. Kang 1989).

It is undeniable that there are similar barbaric moments in Hebrew history. For example, there is the practice of the "ban"—the killing of all persons after the conquest of a village. One should also note the presence of poetic bloodlust in the final verses of Psalm 137. However, when warfare was recorded in Hebrew tradition, there was, paradoxically, often also a conscious attempt to minimize military celebration and self-glorious relishing of victory.

With respect to the conception and role of God, it is common to find in the Hebrew Bible that God is almost exclusively the agent of warfare by means of a miracle. On many occasions, human involvement is virtually excluded or minimized (Ex. 14-15; Judg. 7). The late Jewish work, the Wisdom of Solomon, actually tries to argue the justice of God's violence. In this book, the enemies of Israel had a choice to leave peaceably or respond to less threatening violence before lethal violence would be resorted to (Wisd. of Sol. 19:13-17).

Interestingly, Millard Lind's thesis is that the early pre-monarchical Hebrew ideology of warfare was actually anti-military, precisely because wars were conducted by "miracle." In fact, wars were often "fought" by God alone. Lind argues that this early ideology of wars fought by God, or miraculous Yahweh Wars, was displaced by the development of the monarchy, which brought with it more of the typical ancient Near Eastern militarism and its religious accoutrements (Lind, 1980). As Mendenhall has stated it:

> The glorification of Yahweh as the "divine warrior" who led his people to victory over the kings in the old poetry of the Federation period…(gave)…way to the glorification of a professional warrior for his superior ability to commit murder. The old "heroic" mentality that regarded military successes as a major theme of epic chant returns with a vengeance very soon after the reversion to Bronze Age pagan political organization in Israel. Yahweh was not nearly so reliable a source of "security" as an effective military general. The

theme that rose to such horrendous atrocities during the Assyrian Empire dominates also most of the history of Ancient Israel and Judah. (Mendenhall 1975, 158)

But perhaps this theological shift may have emerged *after* the development of monarchy, and was thus a reflection of its excesses and mistakes (see 1 Sam. 8).

Similarly, in his classic analysis, Max Weber suggests that the "pacifistic patriarchal legends" and the later "pacifistic prophets" (whose message was of destruction by God alone) had their origins in proletarian protests of the monarchy's professionalization of the military (Weber 1967, 100-103).

What is clear is that the Hebrew Bible is notoriously underwhelming as a "national epic literature." It seems bent on disallowing human pride in military accomplishment. With its constant moralistic reminders of mistakes, sins, and failures, the Hebrew Bible is interested in the human need for God, not power. Even David, the most potentially epic figure in the entire historical narratives, is remembered as much for his failures and abuses of power as for his successes. In the later historical revisions in the books of Chronicles, he is condemned as a man with "blood on his hands" (1 Chron. 28:3, cf. Hosea 1:4, where Jehu is condemned for a political assassination that appears to be commanded in 2 Kings 9:7).

THE HEBREW PEACE TRADITION

I would argue that the Hebrew peace tradition developed late and was a result of Israel becoming stateless. This fall of the monarchy began in 597 B.C.E. and was violently completed in 587 B.C.E., when a number of the Hebrew intellectual and political leaders were exiled to the Neo-Babylonian heartland (what is today southern Iraq). Though often minimized in ancient Israelite religious development, I posit that this exile was a central turning point in biblical theology. This is because it engendered the rise of competing strategies of survival for the future of Israel (see Smith-Christopher 1997). These strategies developed out of diverse responses to two questions: "What does it *now* mean to be the people of God?" and "How do we live in exile?"

With respect to the first question, we can cite here the debates between those who advocated violence and those who advocated

151

nonviolence. On the one hand, there were those who wanted the violent and vengeful destruction of the enemies of God (Ps. 137; Jer. 50, 51); on the other hand, there were those who spoke of the people's new role as a "light to the nations," where Jerusalem would become a world center of learning that required world demilitarization and peaceful conversion of weapons to farming tools (Isa. 2).

In response to the second question, how to live in exile, Jeremiah's famous Letter to the Exiles (29) gives advice. He echoes the Deuteronomic exemptions from military service: build houses, marry off your offspring, and plant gardens (see Deut. 20). By recommending those activities that exempt a Jew from fighting, it can be argued that the emphasis here was placed on nonviolent resistance. Further justification for this interpretation is provided by Jeremiah's conclusion to his letter: "Seek the peace of the city where you live–for in its peace you will find your peace."

Is Jeremiah's advice to be understood as applying to the short- or the long-term? Before his untimely death in 1997, John Howard Yoder had speculated that Jeremiah 29 was not so much an interim ethic as the basis for an "exilic ethic" and possibly an exilic ecclesiology of the Christian church (Yoder, personal correspondence and unpublished manuscripts).

NONVIOLENCE AND UNIVERSAL MISSION

The prophet we know only as "Second Isaiah" (that is, chapters 40-55) formulated a doctrine of redemptive suffering for the exiled Israelite peoples which would then be the basis for a *universal renewal of humanity*. This was a renewal not limited only to the restoration of the Israelite peoples themselves, but which also sought to redefine their relationship to their former enemies (Isa. 2; 19:24-25; 49:6). Included in this developing Hebraic theology of nonviolence and universal mission are the following: the stories of Jonah (a *midrash* based on Isa. 49:6); the little book of Ruth's redefinition of "foreigners" (Ruth, a foreigner, gained acceptance and succeeded whereas Hagar, another foreign woman, had been rejected, Gen. 16, 21); and the book of Daniel, particularly in its renunciation of violent resistance in chapter 11 (see Smith-Christopher 1997).

There are important hints that this view of renewal may also be related to the honoring of the "quiet/peaceful one" in Wisdom traditions (see Prov. 11:30; 14:29; 16:32; 17:9; 20:3; 24:15-18; 25:21-22), which is itself related to the Egyptian ideal of the nonviolent wise (Schupak 1993). The Hebrew image of the patient wise one is also honored in the nonviolence and non-vengeful image of the inter-testamental portraits of Joseph and Taxo (see Harrelson 1977; Licht 1961; Collins 1977).

The loss of statehood led some late Hebrew writers to reject state violence—especially a renewed call to Hebrew state violence—and to advocate an embrace of exile as a "calling" rather than a punishment (Jer. 29; Isa. 49:6). Finally, the powerful story of Jonah moves in an entirely new direction. It radically redefines the nature of being the people of God, a people of mission with a message of reconciliation (see Isa. 2 wherein this reconciliation will lead to the destruction of all weapons). The conclusion, then, is that there is not one singular and consistent answer in the Hebrew Scriptures to the problem of war and relations to the enemy. In fact, there are conflicting interpretations of the tradition of violence, even within the canon of the Hebrew texts. Jesus, then, can be identified as standing faithfully in one, but not all, of these differing post-exilic, Hebraic traditions.

Jesus did not create the Hebrew tradition of nonviolence. He stands in this peace tradition with other early rabbinic teachers (cf. R. Yochanon Ben Zakkai in Neusner 1962, 1970). However, Jesus clearly radicalizes Hebrew nonviolence and clarifies its central importance for the character of his movement. If the nonviolence of Jesus, then, was not only consistent with other rabbinic ethical teachings of the time (whether the majority or not), but also clearly intended to establish the basis for an alternative community in the world, how did the followers respond?

CHRISTIAN NONVIOLENCE AND THE EARLY CHURCH

The Apostle Paul continued the peace teaching of Jesus, but Paul couched his ethical expectations of the Christian life in even stronger contrast to imperial Roman polity. The Christian fellowship, in Paul's view, was an alternative fellowship that was, at the same time, an open challenge to the claims of Rome. As Dieter Georgi has suggested: "Paul sees the congregation as a pluralistic model society" (Georgi 1997, 156). Horsley, in a summary statement, noted how many loaded terms Paul chose from Roman political language. Paul gave them a radically Christian alternative reading: "Insofar as Paul deliberately used language closely associated with the imperial religion, he was presenting his gospel ["good news"] as a direct competitor of the gospel ["good news"] of Caeser" (Horsley 1997, 140). Paul wrote his own peace theology in texts such as Romans 12:9-21, often echoing the teachings of Jesus:

> Bless those who persecute you, bless and do not curse them…live in harmony with one another…. If it is possible, so far as it depends on you, live peaceably with all.

From Paul onward, the normative position in the first three centuries of Christianity was to affirm the nonviolence of Jesus (Hornus 1960; Hunter 1992). With the example of Hippolytus (d. 236 C.E.), the apostolic tradition and the Canons clearly reveal this Christian attitude by the early third century:

> The soldier who is of inferior rank shall not kill anyone. If ordered to, he shall not carry out the order…. The believer who wishes to become a soldier shall be dismissed because they have despised God.

> Canon 13: Of the magistrate and the soldier: Let them not kill anyone even if they receive the order to do so.

> Canon 14: Let a Christian not become a soldier: A Christian must not become a soldier…. Let him not take on himself the son of blood. (Hornus 1960, 163)

It is clear that the political implications of this nonviolence were not missed by early Christian writers. Note in the pseudopigraphic "Epistle of Diognetus" the striking ambivalence about matters of state and national pride:

> They dwell in their own countries, but only as sojourners; they bear their share in all things as citizens, and they endure all hardships as strangers. Every foreign country is a fatherland to them, and every fatherland is foreign…. They find themselves in the flesh, and yet they live not after the flesh. Their existence is on earth, but their citizenship is in heaven.

This nonviolent legacy, however, did not last.

Since Ambrose and Augustine, the majority of Christian scholars of Christian ethics have not denied that the Gospel teachings are pacifist. Rather, they have turned to arguments about "responsible" Christian ethics of peace and war; that is, they focus on just war. According to the just war view, Christians must consider ethical arguments to determine whether a particular conflict is just or not and to determine whether, as Christians, they can participate in the conflict. A just war, according to these Christian ethicists, must be waged only by a legitimate authority and only for a just cause. Further, war must be the last resort; non-combatants must not be injured; and weapons used must be able to discriminate. The goal must be peace rather than gain. The literature on the Just War tradition is vast, as befitting the difficulties of the intellectual alchemy that is necessary to transform the nonviolence of Jesus into a call to arms (cf. Ramsey 1968, 1978, 1988; Yoder 1984).

While there are many variations on the notion of a just war, the ethics of the just war have virtually nothing to do with Jesus. This notion would not have been recognized in the first three centuries of Christianity. No one argues that Jesus meant to speak of just wars, and it is clear that St. Augustine was forced to draw heavily on Greek and Roman sources in creating the earliest definitive version of the idea (see Markus 1983). The normative pacifism of the early Church has yet to be overturned as a canon of historical scholarship.

ONWARD CHRISTIAN SOLDIERS

What John Howard Yoder has called "The Constantinian Shift" changed everything. By 311, the famous Edict of Milan made Christianity, among other faiths, openly legal. By 420, "official Christianity" was beginning to officially persecute heresies. By 436, the radical transformation of official Christianity was complete, for by then, *only Christians* could serve in the Roman legions. The Church was then armed with the power of the Roman legions, and nonviolence came to be viewed as a heresy and an occasional prophetic voice. In the West, prophetic voices have rarely been the subject of serious study. However, in medieval sources, these voices are occasionally heard in protest against the Christian preparation for the Crusades. The role of the peace witness in the centuries from Constantine to the beginnings of the Crusades is an area of research which ought to be further investigated. This would include research into the notion of violence among the Byzantine writings of the Eastern Christian tradition.

Christian nonviolence since Constantine, while not exactly an unbroken chain, is certainly traceable in a long series of episodes. These are typically associated with circumstances of marginality and/or a zeal for a return to the pristine teachings of the earliest Church and its simple Gospel. The Crusades provided a major test of Christian nonviolence in the early years of the second millennium. In fact, it is not widely known that Christian advocates of nonviolence actually opposed the Crusades. For example, Pietro Valdes founded the Waldensians, a northern Italian movement that was pacifist in its origins in the twelfth and thirteenth centuries (see Biller 1983; Haines 1981; Cameron 1984). There were also other opponents of crusading. In his groundbreaking study, Throop wrote that:

> Force having failed miserably in efforts to recover the Holy Land, thoughtful and pious men...began to insist that the crusades were misguided efforts. Men of this type, as capable of self sacrifice and martyrdom as the early crusaders, felt that the recovery of the Holy Land could only come through the use of Christ's own methods: the preaching of the gospel. This pacifist missionary ideal, revived during the early thirteenth century, was deeply antagonistic to the militant crusading ideal of the twelfth century, the ideal which Gregory endeavored so valiantly to resuscitate. Out of the extraordinary religious ferment of the fifteenth century there had grown a perception of the disparity between apostolic poverty and ecclesiastical wealth, between the peace preached by Christ and the holy war urged by his vicar. (Throop 1940, 288, cf. Sibbery 1985; Kedar 1984)

The pacifist Cistercian abbott Isaac of L'Etoile, in his condemnation of warfare and crusading, thundered against the formation of the military "Orders" of monks, calling them a *monstrum novum*, a "new monstrosity." Walter Mapp, an Englishman, became a convert to the Christian pacifist cause and also an outspoken critic of the Crusades on the basis that Christ told His disciples to put away their swords. Finally, Peter of Chelcice, who stood on the left wing of the Czech reform movement, provided one of the clearest expressions of pre-Reformation Christian nonviolence when he wrote:

> If St. Peter himself should suddenly appear from Heaven in order to begin to advocate the sword and to gather together an army in order to defend the truth and to establish God's order by worldly might, even then I would not believe him. (Brock 1972, 37-38)

It is significant that Christian nonviolence, particularly during the Crusades, continued to be advocated in the face of the zealous calls for war that used the language of Christianity. In other words, Christian nonviolence continued to be viewed as a form of political atheism. This is also clearly illustrated in examples taken from the histories of the three main "Peace Churches"—those Christian movements for whom nonviolence is a matter of explicit doctrine of faith—the Mennonites, the Church of the Brethren, and the Quakers.

POLITICAL ATHEISM AND THE PEACE CHURCH TRADITION OF CHRISTIAN NONVIOLENCE: MENNONITES, BRETHREN, AND QUAKERS

Among the three Peace Churches are the theological descendants of the Anabaptist movement (Mennonites, Amish, and Hutterites). The Anabaptists were part of the "Radical Reformation." They were so named because they were to the left of the more famous reformers: Luther, Calvin, and Zwingli. The word "Anabaptist" (literally "re-baptizer") derives from early and insistent advocacy of the rite of adult, or "believer's baptism" (that is, baptism as a willed act to accompany a free choice to become a Christian). Rejection of violence was among the earliest doctrinal characteristics of this movement. While infant baptism was considered a symbol of citizenship in a nation-state, re-baptism was interpreted as an act of political atheism. Thus, in re-baptism, there is the powerful symbolism of rejecting the kingdom of this world for an alternative kingdom of Christ. This made the re-baptizers essentially exiles. The Anabaptists themselves consistently spoke in charged political terms about higher loyalties.

With respect to these higher loyalties, in 1527 the attempt was made to lend some kind of formal cohesion to the rapidly growing peasants religious movement. The result was the Schleitheim Confession. The confession clearly stated a position with respect to war and Christian nonviolence:

> Thereby…shall fall away from us the diabolical weapons of violence, such as sword, armor and the like, and all of their use to protect friends or against enemies, by virtue of the word of Christ 'you shall not resist evil.' (Yoder 1977, Article IV)

The Church of the Brethren (often known by their nickname, the "Dunkers" or "Dunker Brethren," a reference to their practice of a believer's baptism by immersion three times in a trinitarian formula), cannot really be considered separately from Anabaptism. The Brethren movement begins circa 1708 with a group in Schwarzenau which was thoroughly acquainted with Anabaptist ideas. The group was also influenced by the renewal movements surrounding German Pietism (increased Bible study, better preaching, emphasis on personal faith, etc.).

Notable among the records of early persecution of the Church of the Brethren is the recorded conversations of John Naas of Nordheim. After Nass refused induction, the King of Prussia asked him:

> "Why will you not enlist with me?" "Because," replied Naas, "I have already, long ago, enlisted into one of the noblest and best of enrollments, and I would not, and indeed could not, become a traitor to Him.... My captain is the great Prince Immanuel, our Lord Jesus Christ. I have espoused his cause and therefore cannot, and will not, forsake him." (Bowman 1941, 54)

Note, once again, the issue of split political as well as theological loyalties in conversation with the state.

Finally, Quakerism grew out of the turbulent, violent events precipitated by the Puritan uprising in England, which culminated in the English Civil War 1642-1645. The Puritan uprising was a reformist movement in the tradition of John Calvin, driven by evangelical zeal and fueled by political anger. A spectrum of ideologies contributed to the Puritan movement that filled the ranks of Cromwell's "New Model Army." Radical Puritans read Daniel and Revelation. They were confident that the Jerusalem described within these texts was not, in fact, the Jerusalem located in the Middle East but was a metaphor for England herself.

The founder of the Quaker sect, George Fox, was the son of a Puritan and the focal point for the convergence of a number of early Quaker leaders. Fox was certainly orthodox in his Christian faith. He laid heavy stress, however, on the implication and modern meaning of the spiritual presence of Jesus Christ—the "inward light" whom Fox referred to as "our present teacher." Certainly, there was a fluidity to early Quaker belief on violence. Not all the earliest Quakers were pacifists; George Fox himself was offered an officer's rank in Cromwell's army. Fox's response to this offer has become a classic statement in Quaker tradition:

> I told them I lived in the virtue of that life and power that took away the occasion of all wars: and I knew from whence all wars did rise, from the lust, according to James. And still they courted me to accept their offer…but I told them I was come into the covenant of peace, which was before all wars and strifes was; and they said they offered it in love and kindness to me, because of my virtue, and suchlike, and I told them that if that were their love and kindness, I trampled it under my feet. (Brock 1972, 259)

Fox's statement is a classic case of political atheism. Fox rejects the mainstrain definitions of Christian faithfulness, loyalty, and action with respect to warfare and opts for an alternative belief and practice. His revolutionary zeal went away from a war with "carnal weapons" and in the direction of a "Lamb's War," a profound early Quaker image derived from Revelation. The concept of the Lamb's War may best be described as a nonviolent, spiritual "Jihad." One early Quaker's witness, when he refused to accept the so-called faith of statecraft and warfare, is instructive:

> Before the first summons came I received a summons from the Prince of Peace to march under His banner, which is love, who came not to destroy men's lives but to save them. And being enlistees under this banner I dare not desert my colors to march under the banner of the kings of this earth. (Brock 1972, 291)

It is appropriate to ask here, Does the Quaker belief system call into question not only direct participation in warfare but also reaping the benefits of warfare? John Woolman, whose *Journals* remain a classic of early American literature, dealt with this question by refusing to wear dyed clothing because most commercial cloth was dyed by slaves. In 1774, Woolman asked Quakers to consider whether the "seeds of war" could be found in the very clothes that they wore (Woolman 1971, 255). More recently, Leonard Friedrich, a German Quaker, was arrested by the Nazis and sent to Buchenwald in 1942 for his "pacifistische judenfreundliche" opinions (the official Nazi SS papers are still in the possession of Friedrich's descendants).

CONCLUDING OBSERVATIONS

The challenge of Christian nonviolence, as we have seen, is not new. Throughout the history of Christianity, we find a persistent criticism of violence and numerous examples of people who actually lived according to their nonviolent beliefs.

Reinhold Niebuhr, the great Christian ethicist of the twentieth century, believed that it was good to have a few pacifists around, the way it is good to have a few saints around. But Niebuhr seriously miscalculated. Pacifists are not otherworldly saints nor are they agreeably quiet museum exhibits of ethical curiosities. Rather, they are heretics. They are atheists who stand against the religion of military gods. As we have demonstrated, it is their willingness to live and die for their beliefs that makes their persistent faith in nonviolence so dangerous to those in power.

It is, after all, one thing to say we will beat our swords into plowshares. Many Christians join hands and say these words about peace with tearful emotion. But when someone actually takes hammer to blade, whether figuratively, by refusing military induction, or literally, as in the case of Father Daniel Berrigan and his friends who broke into arms plants and smashed missile parts with hammers (see Stringfellow and Towne 1971), the crowds turn ugly and frantically try to crush the heresy of political atheism.

It seems hardly necessary to underscore the fact that political atheism does not mean disengagement from the world. In his famous prayer, Jesus recognized that his teaching would lead people to "not belong to the world" (John 17:14); however, he does not ask that his followers be taken out of the world (John 17:15). Jesus advocated care for the sick, the prisoner, the hungry, and the oppressed (Matthew 25:31-46). It is perfectly clear from his admonitions that Christian nonviolence must always be an engaged nonviolence. An alternative interpretation is that Christian nonviolence is a *missionary* nonviolence—which sends its adherents into a violent world to be agents of change and examples of an alternative view of reality.

160 Christianity, which began as a Hebraic movement, retains ethical expectations which are decidedly "this-worldly" (see Epistle of James). The building of alternative institutions—schools, hospitals, various care facilities—are obvious expressions of Christian

radical faith and have always been a part of nonviolent Christian faithfulness in the world (see Gish 1974; Brown 1971; Yoder 1977, 1994; Wink 1984-1992; Borg 1998).

Yet, Christian advocates of nonviolence maintain their skepticism for all purely political solutions to social problems. Jacques Ellul, for example, wrote of the dangers of the "political illusion" (see Ellul 1967) and the Brethren scholar, Vernard Eller, suggested the language of a Christian "Anarchism" (see Eller 1987). Advocates of engaged Christian nonviolence have always struggled with the level of militancy that their passion for justice can engender. Do we resist corruption and set up alternative societies by free choice (Amish) or remain engaged in wider society, always risking compromise? How forceful can that engagement be, yet remain faithful to both nonviolence and liberty of conscience? What happens when our political allies come to power and we find ourselves now confronting their "new" or "liberated" violence, that is just as deadly?

The compelling call of Jesus to a new reality is a call which, as we have shown, is fundamentally radical. This radical faith refuses the call to worldly battles because Christians are already engaged in a different battle:

> For our struggle is not against enemies of blood and flesh, but against the rulers, against the authorities, against the cosmic powers of this present darkness, against the spiritual forces of evil in the heavenly places. Therefore, take up the whole armor of God, so that you may be able to withstand on that evil day, and having done everything to stand firm. Stand therefore, and fasten the belt of truth around your waist, and put on the breastplate of righteousness. As shoes for your feet put on whatever will make you ready to proclaim the gospel of peace. with all of these, take the shield of faith, with which you will be able to quench the flaming arrows of the evil one. Take the helmet of salvation, and the sword of the spirit, which is the word of God. (Eph. 6:12-17)

Political atheism can only be sustained in the presence of radical faith. For Christians to take the wine and bread of solidarity with Christ is to break ranks with the gods of nationalism—it is to renew the call to what the early Quakers christened as "the Lamb's War."

> …but the people who are loyal to their God shall stand firm and take action: The wise among the people shall give understanding to many. (Dan. 11:32b-33a)

BIBLIOGRAPHY

Anderson, Paul. "Jesus and Peace." In *The Church's Peace Witness*, ed. Miller and Gingerich, 104-130. Grand Rapids: Eerdmans, 1994.

Biller, Peter. "Waldensian Adhorrence of Killing, pre. c. 1400." In *Studies in Church History* 20 (1983): 129-46.

Borg, Marcus. *Conflict, Holiness, and Politics in the Teachings of Jesus.* 2d ed. Harrisburg, Pa.: Trinity Press International, 1998.

Bowman, Rufus. *The Church of the Brethren and War, 1708-1941.* New York: Garland, 1941.

Brock, Peter. *The Political and Social Doctrines of the Unity of Czech Brethren.* The Hague: Mouton, 1957.

Brock, Peter. *Pacifism in Europe to 1914.* Princeton: Princeton University Press, 1972.

Brown, Dale. *The Christian Revolutionary.* Grand Rapids: Eerdmans, 1971.

Brueggemann, Walter. *Theology of the Old Testament: Testimony, Dispute, Advocacy.* Minneapolis: Fortress Press, 1997.

Cahill, Lisa Sowle. *Love Your Enemies: Discipleship, Pacifism, and Just War Theory.* Minneapolis: Fortress Press, 1994.

Cameron, Euan. *The Reformation of the Heretics: The Waldenses of the Alps 1480–1580.* Oxford: Oxford University Press, 1984.

Collins, John J. *The Apocalyptic Vision of the Book of Daniel.* Missoula: Scholars Press, 1977.

Cook, Michael. "Jesus and the Pharisees—The Problem as It Stands Today." In *Journal of Ecumenical Studies* 11.

Cogan, Morton. *Imperialism and Religion.* Missoula: Scholar's Press, 1974.

Eller, Vernard. *King Jesus Manual of Arms for the Armless: War and Peace from Genesis to Revelation.* Nashville: Abingdon, 1973.

Eller, Vernard. *Christian Anarchy.* Grand Rapids: Eerdmans, 1987.

Ellul, Jacques. *The Political Illusion.* New York: Knopf, 1967.

Engelhardt, Tom. *The End of Victory Culture.* Amherst: University of Massachusetts Press, 1995.

Finkel, Asher. *The Pharisees and the Teacher of Nazareth.* Leiden: E. J. Brill, 1964.

Finkelstein, Louis. *The Pharisees: The Sociological Background of Their Faith.* Philadelphia: The Jewish Publication Society of America, 1940.

Genot-Bismuth, Jacqueline. "Pacifisme Phariseien et Sublimiation de L'Idee de Guerre aux Origines du Rabbinisme." In *ETR* 1 (1981): 783-89.

Georgi, Dieter. "God Turned Upside Down." In *Paul and Empire: Religion and Power in Roman Imperial Society*, ed. Richard Horsley, 148-157. Harrisburg: Trinity Press International, 1997.

Gish, Art. *The New Left and Christian Radicalism.* Grand Rapids: Eerdmans, 1974.

Haines, Keith. "Attitudes and Impediments to Pacifism in Medieval Europe." In *Journal of Medieval History* 7 (1981): 369-89.

Harrelson, W. "Patient Love in the Testament of Joseph." In *Perspectives in Religious Studies* 4 (1977): 4-13.

Hiller, Kurt. "Linkspazifismus." In *Ratioaktiv, Reden 1914-1964*, 27-49. Limes Verlag, 1966.

Hornus, Jean Michael. *It is Not Lawful for Me to Fight*. Scottdale: Herald Press, 1960.

Horsley, Richard, ed. *Paul and Empire: Religion and Power in Roman Imperial Society*. Harrisburg: Trinity Press International, 1997.

Hunter, David. "A Decade of Research on Early Christians and Military Service." In *Religious Studies Review*, vol. 18, no. 2 (1992): 87-94.

Kang, Sa-Moon. *Divine War in the Old Testament and in the Ancient Near East*. New York: W. de Gruyter, 1989.

Kedar, Benjamin. *Crusade and Mission*. Princeton: Princeton University Press, 1984.

Kimmelman, Reuven. "Non-Violence in the Talmud." In *Judaism*, vol. 17, no. 3 (1968): 316-334.

Klassen, William. *Love Your Enemies: The Way to Peace, Overtures to Biblical Theology*. Philadelphia: Fortress Press, 1984.

Licht, J. "Taxo, or the Apocalyptic Doctrine of Vengeance." In *Journal of Jewish Studies* 12 (1961): 95-103.

Lind, Millard. *Yahweh is a Warrior*. Scottdale: Herald Press, 1980.

Markus, R.A. "Saint Augustine's Views on the `Just War'." In *The Church and War, Papers from the Ecclesiastical History Society*, 1-14. Oxford: Blackwell, 1983.

Marrin, Albert, ed. *War and the Christian Conscience*. Chicago: Henry Regnery, 1971.

Mekhilta of R. Ishmael. Trans. J. Lauterbach. 3 vols. Philadelphia: Jewish Publication Society of America, 1933-35.

Mendenhall, George. "The Monarchy." *Interpretation* 29 (1975): 155-170.

Neusner, Jacob. *From Politics to Piety: The Emergence of Pharasaic Judaism*. Englewood Cliffs: Prentice-Hall, 1972.

Neusner, Jacob. *A Life of R. Yochanon Ben Zakkai*. Leiden: E. J. Brill, 1962.

Neusner, Jacob. *The Development of a Legend: Studies in the Traditions Concerning R. Yochanon Ben Zakkai*. Leiden: E. J. Brill, 1970.

Ollenburger, Ben. "From Timeless Ideas to the Essence of Religion: Method in Old Testament Theology before 1930." In *The Flowering of Old Testament Theology*, ed. Ollenburger, Martin, and Hasel, 3-19. Winona Lake: Eisenbrauns, 1992.

Ollenburger, Ben. Introduction to *Holy War in Ancient Israel*, by Gerhard Von Rad., ed. Marva J. Dawn. Grand Rapids: Eerdmans, 1991.

Pawlikowski, John. *What Are They Saying about Jewish-Christian Relations?* New York: Paulist Press, 1980.

Pawlikoski, John. *Christ in the Light of Jewish Christian Dialogue*. New York: Paulist Press, 1982.

Piper, John. *Love Your Enemies*. Cambridge: Cambridge University Press, 1980.

Polner, M. and N. Goodman. *The Challenge of Shalom*. Philadelphia: New Society Publishers, 1994.

Polner, M. and J. O'Grady. *Disarmed and Dangerous: The Radical Lives and Times of Daniel and Philip Berrigan*. New York: Basic Books, 1997.

Punshon, John. *Portrait in Gray: A Short History of the Quakers*. London: Quaker Home Service, 1984.

Ramsey, Paul. *The Just War: Force and Political Responsibility*. New York: Scribner, 1968.

Ramsey, Paul and R. A. McCormick, ed. *Doing Evil to Achieve Good: Moral Choice in Conflict Situations*. Chicago: Loyola University Press, 1978.

Ramsey, Paul. *Speak Up for Just War or Pacifism: A Critique of the United Methodist Bishops' Pastoral Letter "In Defense of Creation."* University Park: Pennsylvania State University Press, 1988.

Saggs, H. W. F. "Assyrian Warfare in the Sargonid Period." *Iraq* 25 (1963): 149-162.

Schwarzschild, Steven. "Shalom." In *The Challenge of Shalom,* ed. M. Polner and N. Goodman, 16-25. Philadelphia: New Society Publishers, 1994.

Shoeps, H. J. *Theologie und Geschichte des Judenshcristentums*. Tuebingen: Mohr, 1949.

Shupak, Nili. *Where Can Wisdom Be Found? The Sage's Language in the Bible and in Ancient Egyptian Literature*. Fribourg, Switzerland: University Press/Goettingen: Vandenhoeck and Ruprecht, 1993.

Siberry, Elizabeth. *Criticism of Crusading: 1095-1274*. Oxford: Oxford University Press, 1985.

Smith-Christopher, Daniel. "The Book of Daniel." In *The New Interpreter's Bible*, vol. 12. 1996.

Smith-Christopher, Daniel. "Between Ezra and Isaiah: Exclusion, Transformation and Inclusion of the 'Foreigner' in Post-Exilic Biblical Theology." In *Ethnicity and the Bible*, ed. Mark Brett, 117-142. Leiden: E. J. Brill, 1996.

Stringfellow, William and A. Towne. *Suspect Tenderness: The Ethics of the Berrigan Witness*. New York: Holt, Rinehart and Winston, 1971.

Summers, Harry G. "What is War?" In *Harper's Magazine* (May 1984): 75-78.

Throop, Palmer. *Criticism of the Crusades*. Amsterdam: N. v. Swet and Zeitlinger, 1940.

Vermes, Geza. *Jesus the Jew*. 2d ed. London: SCM, 1983.

Vogt. *The Decline of Rome*. London: Weidenfeld and Nicolson, 1965.

Weber, Max. *Ancient Judaism*. Trans. Gerth and Mertindale. Glencoe: Free Press, 1967.

Wengst, Klaus. *Pax Romana and the Peace of Jesus Christ*. Philadelphia: Fortress Press, 1987.

Wink, Walter. *The Powers*. 3 vols. Philadelphia: Fortress Press, 1984-1992.

Womersley, David. *The Transformation of The Decline and Fall of the Roman Empire*. Cambridge: Cambridge University Press, 1988.

Woolman, John. "A Plea for the Poor." In *The Journal and Major Essays*, ed. Phillips Moulton. New York: Oxford University Press, 1971.

Yoder, John Howard. *The Politics of Jesus*. 2d ed. Grand Rapids: Eerdmans, 1994.

Yoder, John Howard. *The Christian Witness to the State*. Newton: Faith and Life Press, 1977.

Yoder, John Howard. *When War is Unjust*. Minneapolis: Augsburg, 1984.

Yoder, Jonn Howard, trans. *The Schleitheim Confession*. Scottdale: Herald Press, 1977.

Yoder, John Howard. "The Constantinian Sources of Western Social Ethics." In *The Priestly Kingdom: Social Ethics as Gospel*, 125-147. Notre Dame: University of Notre Dame Press, 1984.

Zerubavel, Yael. *Recovered Roots: Collective Memory and the Making of Israeli National Tradition*. Chicago: University of Chicago Press, 1995.

Epilogue

REFLECTIONS ON NONVIOLENCE AND RELIGION

by Donald K. Swearer

Subverting Hatred demonstrates two coexistent, seemingly paradoxical truths: (1) the world's religions have not consistently embodied the principles of peace and nonviolence; (2) the world's religions have made significant contributions to the ideals of peace and nonviolence. As the essay on Islam puts this paradox, "The same 'beautiful example' [Mohammed] which inspired the great heroes of nonviolence in Islamic history was also appealed to for justification by the fiercest opponents of these advocates of nonviolence as well;" or from a similar perspective, the challenge faced by Rabbi Jeremy Milgrom to wrestle with the story of violence in the Hebrew scriptures and yet arrive at the conclusion that there is a nonviolent Torah. Each of the essays in distinctive ways acknowledges the problematic relationship religion has to peace and nonviolence and then vigorously pursues the positive contribution made by religion to "subverting hatred." In what ways have the religious traditions represented in this volume contributed to the ideals of peace and nonviolence and can they continue to do so? I propose to examine this question in terms of four interconnected topics addressed in this volume: worldview and practice; symbols and stories; inner peace and world peace; weakness and strength.

DONALD K. SWEARER is the Charles and Harriet Cox McDowell Professor of Religion at Swarthmore College where he teaches courses in Asian and comparative religions and is a member of the Asian Studies and Environmental Studies Programs. He was the Numata Visiting Professor of Buddhist Studies at the University of Hawaii in 1993 and a Guggenheim Fellow in 1994. His publications include *Me and Mine: Selected Essays of Bhikhu Buddhadasa* (1989); *For the Sake of the World: The Spirit of Buddhist and Christian Monasticism* (1989); *Ethics, Wealth, and Salvation: A Study in Buddhist Social Ethics* (1990); *The Buddhist World of Southeast Asia* (1995); and *The Legend of Queen Cama* (1998).

WORLDVIEW AND PRACTICE

Religious traditions embody a worldview and a way of life that flows from that worldview. For example, Christians affirm that because God is love they should love their neighbors as themselves. To be sure, Christians debate both the meaning of neighbor and of love but the principle of neighbor love grounded in a belief in a loving God lies at the very core of Christian ethics and, indeed, of Christian identity. Similarly, as Christopher Queen points out, the Buddhist worldview concepts of not-self, dependent origination, and emptiness undergird the Buddhist ethical value of compassion, and for Sunanda and Yajneshway Shastri, the Hindu view of the ultimate oneness underlying the multiplicity of the visible universe necessarily promotes a nonviolent lifestyle of harmony and mutuality. Because violence contravenes the very nature of reality, it destroys both inner peace and the peace of the world.

To the debate regarding strategies for promoting world peace, the world's religions insist that actions should reflect how one views the nature of the world. The Buddhist insistence that one's way or path in the world begins with "right view" admirably illustrates this point of view. Even though insistence on right view at times has led to doctrinal chauvinism and exclusive claims to truth, the authors of this volume contend that religious worldviews have promoted and continue to promote peace and nonviolence. As the Buddhist Eightfold Path illustrates, understanding the world not in dualistic terms but as the matrix of mutual interdependence entails both not-killing and compassionate regard for the other, be it human, animal, or the earth itself.

My father's frequent admonition to me as a child was, "Do as I say, not as I do." This contradiction is of the same kind as the challenge to the underlying assumption that believing in a loving God leads to loving behavior, or that Daoist naturalism promotes less violent behavior regarding the environment, or that the Buddhist image of the Jeweled Net of Indra promotes mutual understanding and harmony between majorities and minorities. While religious worldviews may indeed be compatible with the ideals of peace and non-violence, the question remains, how does one translate what the text *says* into what one actually *does*, that is to say, how does worldview affect behavior?

The essay on Confucianism and Daoism suggests an answer to this question, namely, that how we live in the world is as much or more a consequence of the communities that form our identities and our participation in communal activities, especially rituals, as it is a shared worldview. The point is a simple one, really, and contradicts my father's comment regarding words and deeds. Much of the time we find ourselves more influenced by the examples and actions of those around us than by what they merely say or, if you will, what the text teaches. As was in fact true in my father's case, actions and words (or texts) should be mutually reinforcing. Tam Wai Lun points out that Mozi and both the Confucian *Analects* and Daoist *Daodejing* support the ideals of peace and nonviolence, but that among the thirteen villages in Fujian Province along the Heyuan River, a major factor in maintaining peaceful relations is not the teachings of texts but the shared worship of their local *jiao* or god, Marquis Hehu, and that among the eight lineages in the Zhongfang region of Jiangxi Province a two-week temple festival honoring their local deity provides a crucial venue for resolving conflicts that arise from competition for scarce resources.

Do the communities in which we live foster the values of harmony, compassion, and nonviolence or, rather, do they promote the opposite—machismo competition, strident self-assertion, and violence? Recent studies of American cultural and social attitudes by Robert Putnam and others reveal a disturbing decline in community participation from PTAs to scouting, a pervasive "bowling alone" cultural mentality. Paradoxically, these studies also point to a yearning for a sense of community belonging, family values, and a less violent society. Each of the essays in this volume insists that true nonviolence does not end with the United Nations Declaration on Human Rights, or a militarily enforced peace in Bosnia and Rwanda—important as these initiatives and programs are— but in the building of communities of mutual regard not simply according to a pragmatic calculus but with a profound sense of the necessary connection between human flourishing and the very nature of the universe we inhabit.

169

SYMBOLS AND STORIES

Symbols and stories are at the very heart of religious communities. Symbols, such as the cross for Christianity, or the dynamic interaction of *yin* and *yang* in the Chinese tradition, or the Hindu mantra, *Om,* convey a multiplicity of meanings that both encompass their traditions and point beyond them. Symbols by their very nature are dynamic and multivalent. The cross symbolizes the seemingly contradictory meanings of the atoning power of self sacrificial love, the imperium of the Holy Roman Empire, or the righteous militancy of the Crusades. The metaphors and narratives that ground a religious community's sense of identity likewise contain multiple meanings. For example, the image of the Buddha seated in meditation under the Tree of Enlightenment may be read as the culminating episode in a story of ascetical withdrawal from worldly concerns, but for contemporary Buddhist environmentalists it represents the imperative to conserve forests in the face of the wholesale degradation of the natural environment. The essays in this volume demonstrate the continuing relevance of religious symbols, master metaphors, and stories to the on-going work of religiously grounded peace activists.

Christopher Queen's reconfiguration of the Wheel of the Law as the Wheel of Peace employs a symbol at the core of the Buddhist tradition to serve the ideals of peace and nonviolence. In early Indian Buddhism a dual meaning is ascribed to the symbol of the wheel: the power of the Buddha's teaching (*dharma*) and the sovereign power of the king. Queen proposes that the Buddha's first teaching, "Turning the Wheel of the Law" transforms the ancient Indian symbol of military conquest associated with the high gods Vishnu and Indra into a metaphor of nonviolence, and that early Indian Buddhist texts draw a picture of the Buddha as a Prince of Peace specifically in opposition to a Lord of War. The same "radical shift in social values" holds true for King Asoka, the greatest Buddhist monarch in the history of Indian Buddhism, whose rule by righteousness called for abstention from killing animals and cruelty to living beings and the positive extension of loving kindness to all sentient beings.

In an even more striking reconfiguration of meaning, Rabia Terri Harris renders the term, Islam, not in its more conventional sense of submission or surrender to the divine will but, through its ety-mological link to *salam* (peace), she proposes a new definition—Way of Peace or reconciliation. In a similar vein, while Harris rec-ognizes the imperialistic significance of *jihad*, often translated as "holy war," she points out that in the Qur'an the term means struggle or effort, especially the establishment of justice, and that the work of nonviolence is the ultimate root of *jihad*. The qualities of struggle and justice central to *jihad* challenge quietistic nonviolence while, at the same time, challenge mainstream Muslim attitudes toward power from the perspective of the Sufi alternative Islamic commu-nity as represented, for example, by the late Guru Bawa Muhaiyadeen: "It is compassion that conquers. It is unity that con-quers.... The sword doesn't conquer; love is sharper than the sword."

The authors of this volume share with their readers stories of figures who personify the ideals of nonviolence, human dignity, peace, reconciliation, and justice. Some appeal to the founders of traditions—Mohammed, the Buddha, Mahavira, Confucius—or classical figures in their histories—White Antelope, Al-Hallaj, Chaitanya, Jinacandras, Rabbi Yochanon Ben Zakkai, but the most compelling are modern exemplars who represent by their very contemporaneity a situational relevance to our times. The figure of Mahatma Gandhi looms large among contemporary exemplars of the nonviolent struggle for human dignity, civil rights, and social justice as does one of his most prominent heirs, Martin Luther King, Jr. Many readers will be introduced for the first time to other lesser known but other notable figures and their work such as: Gandhi's Pathan Muslim contemporary, `Abdul-Ghaffar; B. R. Ambedkar's work among the Dalit untouchable community of India; Acarya Tulsi's nine principles of nonviolence; and the Cheyenne Chief, Lawrence Hart. These exemplary lives are instructive but, more importantly, they demonstrate the ideals of peace, justice, and non-violence not simply as universal principles but as realistic options for how to live in the world.

INNER PEACE AND WORLD PEACE

Peace and nonviolence connote an ethos ordinarily associated with society or the state; however, as suggested by the title of this volume, *Subverting Hatred*, religions have taken an especially strong interest in promoting individual lives of nonhatred, nonviolence, love, and compassion. Whether at the level of the individual or society, the religious witness to the values of peace and nonviolence recognizes both a problematic to be overcome or negated and a goal or way of living in the world to be achieved. For example, the *hadith* acknowledges the most difficult struggle (*jihad*) to be the inward effort of confronting our base nature and sees the equally important but lesser struggle as the outward effort of confronting social injustice. The social consequences of following the Buddhist Eightfold Path—right actions, speech, livelihood—depend on the individual's success in negating hatred, greed, and ignorance. *Santi,* the Hindu term for peace, has a dual meaning: spiritual peace and peace in society and nature. Although spiritual peace is considered to be the highest achievement, it entails overcoming a sense of separateness and identifying with all beings in the universe. In this way *Santi* requires both inner peace and world peace. In various ways, all religious traditions link the transformation of social and political violence to the transformation of inner violence. Put in a more general terms, religious traditions consistently affirm, "A good tree bears good fruit."

Engaged Buddhism as represented, in particular, by the Vietnamese monk, Thich Nhat Hanh, challenges the conventional separation between the individual and the world and it condemns the violent Other that excludes our own connectedness to the world "out there." In his powerful poem, "Please Call Me By My True Names," written after he had heard the news of the rape and murder of a 12-year-old Vietnamese girl by Thai pirates who raided a refugee boat in the Gulf of Siam, Nhat Hanh writes:

> I am the 12-year old girl, refugee
>   on a small boat,
> who throws herself into the ocean after
>   being raped by a sea pirate,
> and I am the pirate, my heart not yet capable
>   of seeing and loving.
>
> Please call me by my true names,
> so I can hear all my cries and my laughs
>   at once,
> so I can see that my joy and pain are one.

Please call me by my true names,
    so I can wake up,
and so the door of my heart can be left open,
the door of compassion.

Jainism offers a striking example of the connection between non-violence as an individual achievement involving a highly disciplined, simple, even ascetical lifestyle and nonviolence in society based on the premise that harm to others injures oneself. All observant Jains affirm the principle of nonviolence (*ahimsa*) although with different lifestyle consequences for monks and laity. Lay persons avoid occupations that harm animals and humans, are vegetarians, and avoid wearing material such as silk because it involves the slaughter of silk worms. Jain monks and nuns follow a more rigorous regime, drinking only boiled water, not walking or sitting where there might be living things, and wearing a mouth mask to prevent breathing in small organisms. While Jain monks tend to lead a cloistered life some, such as Acarya Tulsi, are social activists working for the cause of peace and nonviolence. Tulsi worked tirelessly in India for the uplift of widows and children and the alleviation of tensions between Hindus and Sikhs in the Punjab. Furthermore, his code of ethics to promote peace and nonviolence has a general relevance beyond India.

World peace also requires justice, a theme deeply rooted in "the religions of the Book" (Judaism, Christianity, Islam) although not absent from the other religious traditions represented in this volume. Acarya Tulsi's principles of nonviolence are one example. They include a strong appeal to the theme of justice: "No unjust and oppressive steps should be taken by any person, nation or state against the weak, the oppressed, or colored, or particular castes or communities. Principles of justice, impartiality and humanity should be more and more developed and practiced by every individual, nation, and state."

Since the time of the early church fathers, the mainstream Christian position on war and nonviolence has been the just war option, not the stronger position taken by the Peace Churches (Mennonites, Brethren, Quakers). Just war theory justifies violence to achieve peace under certain conditions (e.g., waged only by a legitimate authority for a just cause, a course of last resort, protection of non-combatants, no weapons of mass destruction, the goal of peace rather than self-aggrandizement). Smith-Christopher challenges the just war option on the grounds that the complexity of modern warfare undermines the possibility of determining whether or not a war is just.

Most Muslim scholars from the post-Prophetic period to the early modern period, considering conflict inevitable, fashioned a just war view based on the historical precedent of Mohammed's life and the Qur'an. Legalistic arguments centering on technicalities did not question the basic concept of the just war. Not unlike the position Smith-Christopher holds regarding Christianity, Rabia Terri Harris's chapter sees medieval Muslim theories of war not as an attempt to struggle with the question of justice and nonviolence but as rationalizations of imperial "facts on the ground." She finds both an aggressively militant attitude toward *jihad* and a liberal assertion of peace, tolerance and defensiveness to be inadequate. Harris proposes a more spiritual alternative that places greater emphasis on *jihad* as inner struggle: "Be in a state of God's peacefulness and try to give peace to the world…When you exist in the state of God's actions and conduct and then speak with Him, that power will speak with you" (Guru Bawa Muhaiyaddeen).

The conflict between the state of Israel and the Palestinians offers a particularly difficult challenge to advocates of the pursuit of peace by nonviolent means and modern Jews. Jeremy Milgrom does not shy away from this challenge. Beginning with the prophet Isaiah as his text, he argues that peace and justice are integrally connected, but that peace depends on justice and not the other way around: "Peace without justice is surrender." Transforming Isaiah's eschatological context to contemporary Israel with the help of Mishnah Avot, Milgrom proposes that a just solution to this conflict might be adjudicated by applying the principle of *takanat hashavim* (ordinance of compassionate justice in the restoration of misappropriated property) as a basis to restore property built by Palestinians involuntarily surrendered before 1948 and as a formula for allowing Jews to retain abandoned Arab property. Rabbi Milgrom acknowledges that such a legal solution has less chance of success when the participants lack a shared religious belief in God's ultimate authority, but hopes that an "inspired United Nations dedicated to human and environmental survival" might serve as a functional equivalent. Even if such a legal agreement were to be worked out, however, one wonders whether such a justice could be the basis of true *shalom* (peace)—an ethical totality that subsumes all human virtues and values, truth, justice, righteousness, and grace.

WEAKNESS AND STRENGTH

The paradox of weakness and strength lies at the very core of the power of nonviolence. Gandhi, referred to by the news commentators of his day as a "little brown man in a loin cloth," brought the might of the British colonial empire to its knees. The Gandhian legacy of strength in weakness, furthermore, inspired movements of nonviolent social change throughout the world from Vietnam to the United States. The civil rights struggle of the 1960s in the United States embodied not only commitment to the constitutional value of universal, guaranteed individual rights, but also the Christian ideals of self-sacrificial love and forgiveness. The Gandhian paradox of strength in nonviolence became the paradox of agapic love that brought down the principalities and powers of segregation.

Throughout history the strongest advocates of peace and nonviolence have often spoken from the periphery of political and economic power. For Daniel Smith-Christopher, the very marginality of the peace churches within the Christian tradition—Mennonites, Brethren, Quakers—represents their power. The just war position of the Christian mainstream may contribute to policy debates, but must inevitably compromise with the power of *realpolitik*. Since "The Constantinian Shift" in the fourth century, nonviolence essentially became a Christian heresy despite its legitimacy during the preceding three centuries when the church stood at the political margins. The Christian peace churches adhere to a higher vision of "subverting of hatred" beyond the promises of military solutions, political guarantees, and legal warrants. When George Fox, the early Quaker leader, was offered an officer's rank in Cromwell's army he responded, "I told them I lived in the virtue of that life and power that took away the occasion of all wars." The uncompromising stance of the peace churches on nonviolence upholds a standard that exposes the limits of a more pragmatic, realistic peace witness. Paradoxically, the radical demand of the peace churches at the margins both judges the limits of the just war position and, at the same time, empowers the peace testimony of mainstream Christian churches.

The paradox of strength in weakness finds expression in other religious traditions, as well, perhaps none so dramatically as in the Jains for whom, as detailed by Christopher Chapple, not only nonviolence but also nonpossession lies at the very center of their religious identity. Jains have exerted an influence far beyond their numbers but their influence stems, in part, from their radical adherence to the value of nonviolence. Daoism's classic text, the *Daodejing* highlights the truth of strength through weakness, and action through nonaction. It celebrates the emptiness of valleys rather than the majestic power of mountains, and the natural flow of the universe rather than assertive dominance over it. When asked to become part of the political mainstream, the Daoist philosopher, Zhuanzi, replied that he'd prefer being a turtle dragging its tail in the mud. In conventional terms, weakness and marginality imply insignificance or ineffectiveness and yet both Jains and Daoists have made major contributions to the discourse of peace and nonviolence in India and China.

Among engaged Buddhist leaders, the Dalai Lama, Nhat Hanh, Daisaku Ikeda, Mahaghosananda, and Sulak Sivaraksa stand out as spokespersons for the nonviolent resolution of conflict, world peace, human rights, and social justice. Despite his international visibility, the Dalai Lama lives in exile from his homeland. His power resides in his moral witness rather than temporal strength—a position from which he speaks tirelessly on the themes of compassion and love of enemies and for peace and justice. In his 1989 Nobel Peace Prize acceptance speech, he outlined a Five Point Peace plan as a framework for a negotiated settlement with the People's Republic of China that calls for the transformation of Tibet into a Zone of Nonviolence (*ahimsa*); for China to end its policy of ethnic cleansing; for respecting the fundamental human rights and democratic freedoms of Tibetans; and for restoring and protecting Tibet's natural environment. The Dalai Lama's vision for peace and justice in Tibet has yet to be realized but His Holiness continues his nonviolent struggle in the hope that eventually his moral vision will bear political fruit.

Subverting Hatred demonstrates that religious traditions should not be seen, as Daniel Smith-Christopher argues, to be merely an annoying distraction in contemporary peace and conflict studies. Religious traditions—their worldviews, symbols, stories, and rituals—and their culturally embedded histories provide a critical resource for this field of study and for the practical working out of peacemaking issues. The essays in this volume begin to explore the variety of ways in which religions have both legitimated violence and sanctified nonviolence, justified war and, at the same time, valorized peace. The essays also demonstrate that while issues of war and peace, conflict and reconciliation are, indeed, matters of nation-state and of treaties and law they are ultimately human matters. As Daisaku Ikeda affirms, the final solution to war, violence, and conflict requires a transformation of the vision of what it means to be truly human. In the best sense, religious traditions offer such a vision.